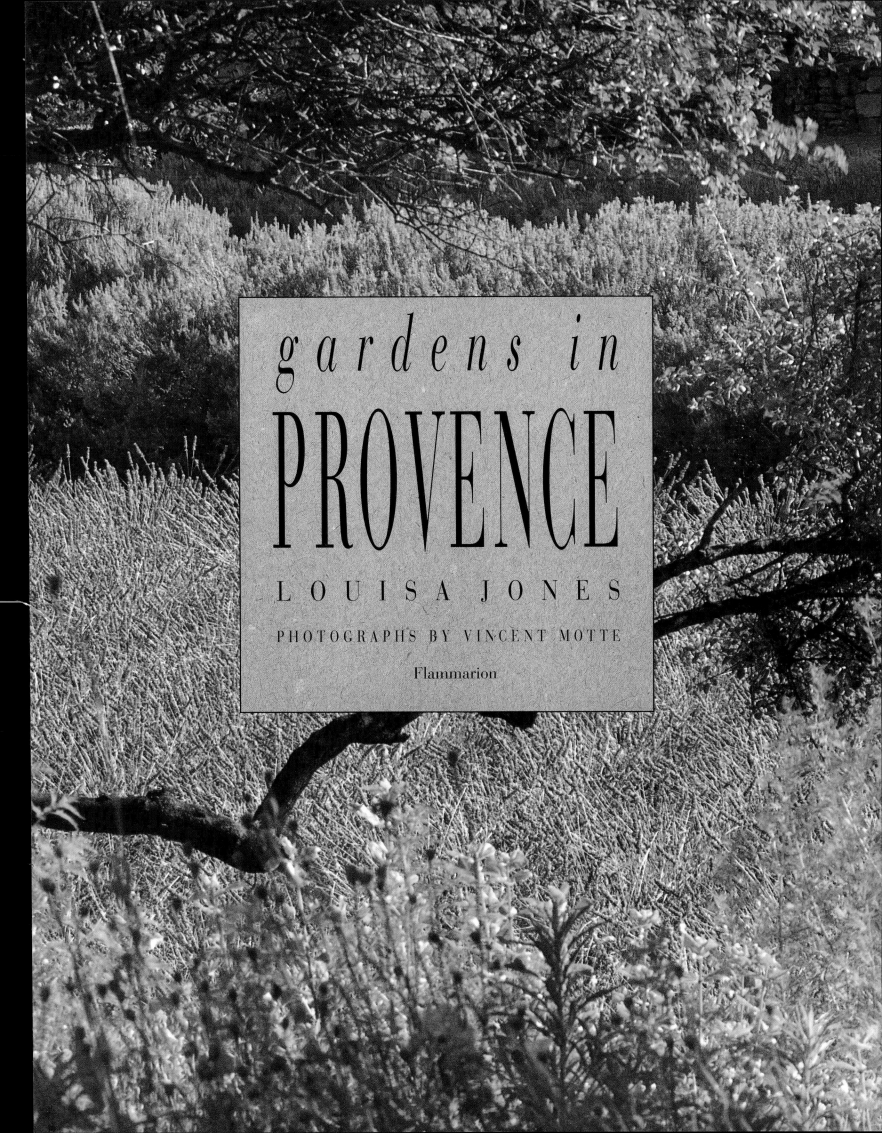

gardens in
PROVENCE

LOUISA JONES

PHOTOGRAPHS BY VINCENT MOTTE

Flammarion

To my grandfather Allen,
who celebrated in his books the spirit
of another place, Arcadia. . . .

Design by
Marc Walter

Copyediting by
Julie Gaskill
Composed by
Octavo Editions, Paris
Photoengraving by
Colourscan France
Map by
Léonie Schlosser
All photographs are
by Vincent Motte, except those
on the following pages by Louisa Jones:
p. 20; p. 37; p. 48 (top); p. 72-73; p. 107; p. 112 (top); p. 113;
p. 119; p. 122 (bottom); p. 127 (bottom); p. 158; p. 171 (top and
bottom); p. 178; p. 179; p. 186; p. 203 (top and bottom); p. 238.

Numéro d'édition : 1089
ISBN: 2-08013-523-6
Printed in Italy by A.G.M

CONTENTS

PREFACE

This book arose quite simply from the union of two passions: the first for Provence, where I have lived for nearly twenty years, and the second for gardens. Initially, I hoped only to share my pleasure through description, though I brought to this venture training as a research scholar. I soon discovered, however, that different publics had varying notions as to the very nature of my subject; that local opinion, Parisian and cosmopolitan expectations varied considerably, that even among expert geographers and historians, quite disparate accounts could be found. Many still question the very existence of a gardening tradition in Provence! I therefore found myself defining a regional style, with all the generalizations that must entail.

As a result, I have tried to base my conclusions directly on my own observations as much as possible, culled over a five-year period in which I visited some two hundred gardens. I must therefore beg the indulgent reader, whose cherished convictions may well be challenged, to regard this essay as an invitation to further exploration, full of delightful surprises.

" The cypress is always occupying my thoughts;
it is as beautiful in line and proportion as an Egyptian obelisk,
and the green has a quality of high distinction;
it is a splash of black in a sunny landscape...." Vincent Van Gogh.

THE HEART
OF PROVENCE

Few parts of the world have been so often or so lovingly portrayed as Provence. Since the early nineteenth century, when French Romantics sought Mediterranean local color and English aristocrats started wintering on the Riviera, the countryside of this region has delighted travelers with an eye for landscape. The coast developed its own character, quickly cosmopolitan; the back country of the pre-Alps became famous for its wild and austere majesty. But the heart of Provence, the lower Rhône valley, while offering an incomparable range of sites—Roman monuments casually slumbering among fragrant shrubbery, cubist hilltowns, labyrinthine grottoes and eerie silver peaks—is largely farmland, pasture and field, cultivated since prehistoric times.

Writers have repeatedly celebrated this region as an earthly Eden. One eighteenth-century traveler extols it unreservedly as "one Great Garden": "The fields and cultivated hills are stor'd with Vines, Almonds, Olives, Figs, Oranges and Pomegranates: and the Wast Ground (if I may so call it) is overspread with Rosemary, Time, Marjoram, Lavender, Myrtil, and divers other odiferous and medicinal Plants. In a word, it's the most fruitful and delectable Province on this side of the Alps, and justly stiled the Paradise of France." British novelist Lawrence Durrell, in *Spirit of Place*, considers it "one of the enchanted landscapes of the human heart." Surprisingly, however, the gardens of Provence are as obscure as its scenery is famous. For though the elegant "bastide" manor houses near Aix and Marseille have attained some recognition, gardens of the lower Rhône valley have been virtually ignored by even the most recent publications. And yet six thousand years of harmony with the earth have created an original blending of agriculture and horticulture that is deeply rooted in the logic of the land. Subtle modulating of foliage and stone, strong formal design, wild gardens, even "edible landscaping"—all these current trends have been known here for centuries. Today, connoisseurs are wedding Mediterranean custom with sophisticated horticultural experimentation to produce extremely original gardens in great variety.

The term "Provence" has meant many things to many people, from the Romans (who invented it as a nickname for their favorite "province") to the present day. For the ancients it extended to the Pyrenees, for many moderns it includes the Côte d'Azur but nothing west of the Rhône. Alphonse Daudet, living near Fontvieille while writing his famous *Letters from My Mill*, situated himself "in the Valley of the Rhône, in the very heart of Provence, on a hill all wooded with pines and oaks, wild vines, mosses and rosemary." His range overlaps with Van Gogh's, by now celebrated to the point of cliché. The Provence explored in this book includes their country and more, corresponding roughly to the lower Rhône valley. This is also, approximately, the area tattooed on the belly of one Pepe, Lawrence Durrell's local guide to the "true" Provence, a man so in love with his land that he keeps it, ambiguously but appropriately, somewhere between heart and stomach. Although the region thus defined includes part of the Rhône's west bank, strictly speaking belonging to Languedoc, it has considerable uniformity in topography, climate and traditions.

Throughout this area, for example, one finds the same layering of cultivation according to altitude. Valleys shelter the choicest crops—strawberries and melons, all sorts of vegetables, flowers for seed companies, fine apples and pears grown on espaliered trees hardly larger than vines elsewhere. All are protected from the fearful north wind by hedges of cypress, bamboo or poplar on one and sometimes two sides. As one moves onto higher, drier ground, cherry and apricot orchards proliferate, yielding to and sometimes overlapping with olive groves and vineyards. Beyond this lie the rocky *garrigue* and maquis, land too dry and too steep to farm, good for pasture, hunting and foraging.

Another unifying factor is the presence everywhere of similar human vestiges: numerous Roman ruins mark the intensity of that civilization's shaping of the land; fragments of medieval castles stand on almost every hilltop,

The vineyards of the south,
"like a pledge that the enchanted landscapes of the European
heart will always exist. . . . " Lawrence Durrell.
Here vineyards and orchardslay against the crags of the Dentelles de Montmirail.

surrounded or not by a village; tiny, elegant Romanesque chapels sit alone by many country roads; châteaux by the dozens, hidden down long avenues of trees. . . . This is a region that contrasts valley and mountain living, with spreading farmsteads below, among a colorful patchwork of fields. Where the nearby slopes have been claimed for habitation, they are topped by picturesque hilltowns.

Such is the Provence best known to the outside world. At the same time, however, its impressive internal diversity can be overlooked and unappreciated by casual visitors. People born here know that just over the crest of the next hill, or beyond the river, lies a completely different country. The silver crags of the Alpilles dominate cypress fields, vineyards and olive orchards dotted with Roman ruins; the steep wooded walls of the Luberon shelter fortified villages with celebrated names; piney red Cézanne country south of the Durance, around Aix, is graced by refined country estates; the irrigated and manicured plains of the Comtat Venaissin spread under the white cone of Mont Ventoux; the jagged peaks of the northern Dentelles de Montmirail display extensive lavender fields and vineyards; the dry scrub country of the Gard, where the plateaux crest like low waves, hide elegant, little-known villages and fortified farms. Fifty kilometers in any direction can mean a change in the cuisine, the local language, the outlook. This is a country of microclimates: on the south slopes of the Alpilles, wild thorny broom flowers all winter while on the north side, just a few minutes away, it heralds the coming of spring. Undoubtedly, diversity within a general pattern is one key to Provence's charm: all its farms, villages, châteaux and cities are similar, and each is impressively unique. All contribute to the character of this rich heartland, which stands in strong contrast both to coastal Provence and the poorer, higher Alpine back country.

These appealing landscapes are small-scaled,

The countryside of Provence
intermingles cultivated fields with wilder hillsides for dramatic effects.
The stony garrigue has been used
for pasture land and foraging since ancient times.

and human. They will not satisfy those who wish to tread on virgin soil or lose themselves in the immensity of mountains, ocean or canyons. In 1935, British novelist Ford Madox Ford suggested in *Provence* that for the man of the Midi "nature is a matter of little squares in the orange, sun-baked earth." This is, he says simply, "land that has been loved—of which every clod . . . [is] as familiar to you as your children and the names of your saints, bullfighters and poets. The sun rises and scorches your limbs whilst you prune your vines; your throat knows the stimulation of the juice of your own grapes that you have pressed, of the oil of the olives you have gathered and crushed, of the herbs you have grown in the mess of pottage of your own beans, of the cheese whose whey was pressed from the milk of your own goats. . . ."

This image of Eden implies an intimacy with the land, carefully and lovingly nurtured through generations of family farming. It is not just a poet's—or an Englishman's—dream: in the lower Durance valley and the Comtat Venaissin, in the mid-1970s, farms of less than ten acres still represented about two-thirds the total number, covering more than forty percent of the territory. Today in the Vaucluse department, there are 13,000 family farms with an average of twenty-four acres. It is the careful attention of these people that creates a countryside so attractive to outsiders that it can be called, in the jargon of contemporary geographers, "a refuge space" for northerners. These scholars wonder if Provençal farmers may have no other future than to become caretakers and gardeners of fine scenery. Many today survive by taking on other jobs as well, often in a nearby city.

When people from Provence praise its gardenlike appearance, they are generally referring to this small-scaled, intensive agriculture. The President du Conseil Générale of the Vaucluse, Jean Garcin, considers his department "the most beautiful garden in France"—thanks

*These landscapes have a human scale,
and still shelter an exceptionally high proportion
of intensely cultivated small farms.*

14

to orchards and fields that produce 25 percent of the fruit and 40 percent of the produce of the region. He adds, "Who would not envy us such a paradise?" Such judgements suggest an ease and grace, a richness of texture, a quality of life that provides pleasure for all the senses, in all seasons—and draws millions of visitors yearly. Permanent plantations such as vines and orchards cover about 20 percent of the region's cultivated land (elsewhere in France only 5 percent); the rest is given to specialized truck farming mainly for vegetables, but also for flowers, seeds and trees. The southern sun allows crops unavailable in the north: olives, almonds and figs, although now the main cash crop, in the Vaucluse, at least, is . . . apples, as it should be in Eden.

This landscape has been so painstakingly shaped and tended that it easily seems "one great garden." And yet, there is also wilderness in Provence. Historian Fernand Braudel comments in *L'Identité de la France* on the southern preponderance of barren or deserted ground (the *saltus* of medieval times, as opposed to cultivated fields, called *ager* by geographers). "A Northerner," he says, "is stupefied, even put off, by these seemingly empty spaces with their bare stone, their scrub growth, their cicadas, their wildlife, and the fragrance of their wild herbs." This is the famous *garrigue* or maquis, stony landscapes of aromatics and low evergreen brush, so fragrant that Napoleon is reported to have said he could recognize his Corsican version blindfolded. Natural historians categorize both *garrigue* and maquis in a number of ways according to cycles of vegetation, soil acidity, plant distribution and size, and do not always agree on the usage of these terms. But all concur on their rocky barrenness.

Relatively unkempt, these rough hills nonetheless provide important resources for human life. Wilderness for the Provençal peasant is an extension of the social community, not its alternative nor its enemy. Scrubland is not uncharted

For novelist Ford Madox Ford, this is simply a country "of which every clod has been turned sedulously and every branch carefully pruned, until you love your bit of land as a child whose every mental change you have followed."

space where a man may free himself from social constraints; rather, like cultivated land, it provides natural resources that only long-accumulated human experience can appreciate. These hills too dry and stony for cultivation provide mushrooms, wild asparagus, game of all kinds, berries, truffles for those who know where to look, firewood, and much, much more.

When regionalist poet Frédéric Mistral recalled childhood days in the mid-nineteenth century, he remembered with some fondness being sent to school in an abandoned monastery in the Montagnette (Saint-Michel de Frigolet, which today houses monks again). In his *Memoirs*, Mistral lovingly described this "lonely and fearsome place," but he also enumerated the resources it afforded for human subsistence —or pleasure: "The surrounding hills were covered with thyme, rosemary, asphodel, box-wood and lavender. There were several small vineyards, which as a matter of fact produced a renowned vintage, the wine of Frigolet; several patches of olive trees planted in the bottom of the valleys; several rows of crooked, blackened almond trees, stunted by the rocky soil; several wild fig trees growing in the clefts of the rock. That was all the cultivated land scattered about that mass of hills. The rest was nothing but waste-land and rubble, but how good it smelled! As soon as the sun shone, we were intoxicated by the fragrance of the mountains." The poet and his comrades spent their days rolling happily in clumps of thyme, gleaning almonds or green grapes, gathering mushrooms underneath the thistles and setting snares for birds. The Monta-gnette has preserved its character even today; picnickers, bicyclists, hikers and botanists barely disturb its solitude on Sundays.

Both wild and farmed land were similarly exploited in Neolithic times. Even then, all over the Mediterranean world, the economy was based on a triad juxtaposing plowed land (for grain crops), shrubby cultures such as the vine and the olive tree, and pasture land for sheep and goats. It cannot be said that man's efforts have always benefited the landscape, however, and the picturesque *garrigue* came into existence through much misuse. In those far-off days, the earliest flocks were led to the mountains for summer grazing, consuming all vegetation along the way. Already the first farmers burned land to clear it for cultivation. Medieval monks and peasants bared hilltops, and their slopes were too steep to hold the topsoil once exposed. Cot-tage industries such as charcoal burning and glassmaking consumed huge quantities of wood. Forest fires still destroy about one hundred thousand acres of forest land in Provence annually. Thus emerged a land with much dra-matically bared rock—though also, of course, a great variety of specially adapted plants. The silva or forest has suffered, perhaps irremedia-bly, in Provence. *Saltus* and *ager* remain, transformed by millennia of human activity. The result is above all a landscape profoundly shaped by human hands, and in that sense, those who speak of the whole landscape as a garden are not wrong.

Many plants today are equally at home on scrubby hillsides, in cultivated fields and in gardens, particularly the olive tree and the winter-flowering rosemary.

ELEMENTS

The Provençal paradise was created by man, for man. Even wildest nature in the Mediterranean world is never raw nor unobserved—yet it must not be thought that it is tamed or subdued. Frequently violent, it can affect crops for years to come with a five-minute hailstorm. The Mediterranean climate hardly seems the gentle air of heaven when it conflicts, as it does constantly, with human efforts. Its universal reputation as a land of leisure notwithstanding, Provence is an Eden of hard toil.

Writers have helped create a popular image of easy living in a land of *far niente*. Alphonse Daudet claimed to get inspiration for his famous Provençal tales, written for Parisian audiences, by consulting "the cicada's library"—on his back in the shade at siesta time. But gardeners arriving from other parts of the world soon discover a harsher reality. "How excessive you all are in Provence," exclaimed Madame de Sévigné

in an oft-quoted complaint to her son-in-law, the Count of Grignan. "Everything is extreme, your heat, your breezes, your north wind, your unseasonable rains, your autumn thunderings: nothing there is gentle or temperate: your rivers overflow, your fields are drowned and spoiled." Nature in Provence is rarely easygoing, and always has the last word.

The general pattern arises naturally from

The Romans planted fruit trees in their wheat fields and vineyards, a custom that persisted in the south until the advent of modern machinery. Still today a cherry or peach tree often graces a Provençal vineyard.

the elements of climate and topography—
simple, basic invariables that farmers and gardeners alike must accept. "Elements" means
weather, of course, but also the raw materials
or building blocks of both landscape and garden
harmonies, inseparable in local tradition. Sun,
water, wind, stone, earth and vegetation have
each their particular characteristics and traditional roles to play.

Provence is famous first and foremost for its
sunshine. "All the beauty of this Provençal
countryside is born of the sun," wrote Daudet.
"It lives by light." Provence is today much tout-
ed in modern advertising for this deity, which
shines on an average of 299 days year in Nice,
for 201 in Paris. (Average summer temperatures
in Avignon are a pleasant 24° centigrade.) The
freeway network, the Côtes du Rhône wines, the
local fabrics are all promoted with the blessing
of Apollo. Even Mistral called his homeland the
Empire of the Sun. And Van Gogh, with his
usual fervor, told his brother Theo: "Oh! those

who don't believe in this sun here are real infi-
dels." Its warmth has been called the south's
most precious natural resource, for the wines
have naturally a higher degree of alcohol than
in the north, the vegetables are sweeter and
more flavorful, the herbs more pungent.

Yet one observes here as in other hot climates that locals avoid the heat of the day.
There is a kind of squaring off, at least in older
generations, between the tanned and the pale,
those who dress up to go to market and those
who undress almost altogether. Windows are
small in traditional Provençal dwellings as in
southern churches, where northern Gothic's
predilection for replacing walls with colored
glass was unthinkable. When Frédéric Mistral
created his epic heroine Mireille, a young maid-
en loyal in love to her young basket weaver, he
imagined her dying (like a Provençal Juliette)
of sunstroke.

Traditional strategies to flee the summer sun
are legion in the south. Not just any shade will

*The Provençal climate also includes
"this taut, wind-hunted sky where the mistral rumbles and screams
all winter long." Lawrence Durrell.*

do—connoisseurs have definite preferences. Some trees must be shunned, like the walnut, and it is said that he who sleeps in the shadow of an oleander will never wake up. The mulberry plane (*mûrier-platane* in French), has become a much-appreciated patio tree for its canopies of large, fresh foliage and its willingness to be pruned. Chinese mulberries are also treasured. Lindens (sometimes called limes), horse chestnuts, and the majestic *Celtis australis* (variously called hackberry or locust) provide the highest and densest canopies, with *Sophora japonica* in the areas close to central France. Elms once spread their generous canopies here, as elsewhere.

Like the sun, water creates and destroys. It can rain a lot in the south: the average annual precipitation can be four to five times that of the Parisian basin, but there are only 50 to 70 wet days a year. Such driving rain, instead of soaking slowly into the ground, carries the top-

soil away. Most of this downpour falls in autumn, October being the wettest month. Only about 15 percent comes between May and August. If unreliable, however, rain is still much solicited. Mistral recounted the pilgrimage of Saint-Anthime in which a procession of farmers leads the saint's statue to the fields to pray for rain; if none is forthcoming, he is dunked three times in the irrigation ditch.

Until modern times, large rivers could be as violent as the heavens. Nearby farmhouses had special barns on the first story where livestock could shelter if there was enough warning. Willa Cather and Henry James both witnessed the Rhône in flood, like Rabelais long before them. Water easily becomes an obsession in Provence, for its excess or its absence. The battle is always to contain its violence and direct its flow, to find it or to keep it away, to store it, to direct it, to navigate it.

Provençal literature contains many tales of stopped-up springs and stolen water—no wealth is worth more. This is in spite of the fact that there has traditionally been a good supply in the lower Rhône valley—the Alps normally provide a wonderful reservoir. Irrigation canals from the Durance were established in the Middle Ages, then regularly extended from the sixteenth to the eighteenth centuries. In the nineteenth, progress was spectacular: in the department of the Bouches-du-Rhône alone, between 1830 and 1913, the amount of irrigated land increased from 500 acres to 100,000. Seasonal extremes of flood and drought remained unconquered however until the 1950s, when the Electricité de France and the Canal of Provence created new dams, sixteen hydroelectric plants, and extensive distribution systems.

Southerners would love to control and direct the wind as they have the rivers, particularly that northern blast called the mistral. Statisticians say that this terrible but tonic scourge, that "health-giving flail" as Ford Madox Ford called it, blows strongest in December, then in March, and finally, in July. Local lore claims that it blows for three-day periods, or multiples of three. The mistral produces brilliant blue skies, tricking the unwary into thinking that

*The Fontaine-de-Vaucluse
is the source of the Sorgue river, which is famous for its sudden shifts
from placid pool to rushing torrent.
Petrarch tried to garden here, but the "river nymphs" would not allow it.*

better, warmer weather has arrived; in summer, of course, the cooling effect can be quite welcome—if there are no forest fires to be whipped out of control. The south wind from the Mediterranean brings rain, except for the summer sirocco that can be particularly hot and desiccating.

Before steam, wind was a major resource: mills were erected as early as the ninth century, again in the twelfth and after the Renaissance. Today, they can be spotted as small, round buildings on hilltops. If such towers are sheltered, and near habitations, they are dovecotes; but if they sit in the force of the wind, they are old mills, even if they have lost their roofs and sails. Daudet claimed to write from such a shelter, ruined after the advent of steam. The works of "his" haven at Fontvieille may be visited, and a table preserves the local names not just for the mistral but for a good thirty others. Other mills complete with their sails stand near Barbentane and Goult.

All writers want to catch the mistral with their words, which have more power here than pictures. Strabo wrote in 64 B.C.: "It is claimed that this wind can move huge stones and that it can, with its breath, throw men off their carts, stripping them of their weapons and clothing." And Colette, in 1927: "If I had persisted in sleeping out of doors, that powerful mouth that breathes coldness and drought, deadens all scents and anesthetizes the earth, the enemy of work, voluptuousness and sleep, would have torn off me the sheets and blankets that it knows how to twist into long rolls. What a strange tormentor, as intent on man as any wild beast!"

Farmers and gardeners seek shelter through the creation of microclimates. One Englishman planted trees so successfully to protect precious shrubs (often personally imported from England) that he could point with pride, on a day of lusty mistral, to his cigarette smoke rising straight up in the air.

Such protection may occur naturally on the southern slopes of the long banks of hard limestone that became the "little mountains" of Provence (rarely more than 2,000 feet), formed

over one hundred million years ago. When the Mediterranean receded from the Rhône and Durance valleys more than twenty million years ago, it left behind the deposits that became the famous "Midi building stone." Lawrence Durrell described its range with his usual verve as "a dozen soft shades from the brown of dried tobacco or coffee to the violets and pearl-pinks of cooling lava—shades of nacre and bistre and honey according to the stoop of the sun." The Roman Pont du Gard was built with blocks from the quarries at Vers that still do business all over France for the construction of fireplaces, benches, and tombstones.

Soil in Provence generally has a very high lime content. Political historians like to speak in terms of red and white Provence, but the earth offers the same contrast: while the powdery white dominates, there are pockets of striking red soil. This rubification, due to the effects of iron oxide and in some cases producing

*A village fountain, explains Provençal
writer Henri Bosco, provides water that "climbs as easily as sap in the veins
of plants; water which you
don't just drink, but which you taste like wine . . . "(opposite).
Hidden quarries can be discovered
off many a country road, more than a hundred in the Vaucluse alone.
The flamboyant ocher beds
in Roussillon draw many visitors every year (above).*

bauxite, is attributed to the soil's degradation. Sites where it is found are usually stunning. Best known is the village of Roussillon, which long lived from its ocher mines, but pockets of similar coloration can be found all over the area, with a large and dramatic concentration near Rustrel.

Such soil is poor, but southerners have had, for millennia, a major asset for soil improvement: their flocks of sheep. The biennial migration of flocks (or transhumance, now largely carried on by truck) has left traces of many *drailles*, or drovers' trails, around Arles and Saint-Rémy, and some of the area's finest gardens lie along them. Today this resource has largely disappeared (although one ambitious gardener is said to have imported sheep manure from England!).

If the region's mostly high alkalinity proves daunting, garden inspiration can be found in the great variety of specially adapted *garrigue* plants with their evergreen or evergray foliage.

There is a wide spectrum of wild vegetation for all soils, even among the trees (always small-scaled too, of course, and generally standing with a strong southern lean): pines (Aleppo, parasol, maritime, Corsican especially); oak (holm, cork, white, kermes, *Quercus ilex*, *Q.suber*, *Q.pubescens*, *Q.coccifera*); hackberry or *Celtis australis*, gleditsias (called "snail trees" in Provence), the wild sumac *Rhus coriaria* and the more recent honey locust (*Robinia pseudoacacia*) spreading fast in some areas. Chestnuts (both castanea and aesculus) are commonly cultivated in higher areas, while linden, fig, plane and mulberry trees (first introduced to feed silkworms when this was a successful cottage industry) are in general use. Travelers are often surprised to find large specimens of what they take to be birches around southern cities and in valley furrows, but these in fact are a kind of poplar (*Populus alba*), with a similar but duskier bark, at home in the Mediterranean plains.

The parkland surrounding old châteaux, as at the Château du Martinet, contains many typical plants: white and green oaks, box and laurustinus, and of course an elegant avenue of plane trees. Stands of bamboo are vestiges of nineteenth-century exoticism.

Native shrubs are in richest profusion in the *garrigue*, which takes its name from the Celtic word for oak; indeed, variants of this landscape are decided by what type of scrub oak dominates the vegetation. Other *garrigue* plants include box, rock rose, myrtle, junipers (including the wonderful "cade" with its pungent wood that cats love), brooms and gorses, roses, viburnums, mastics (related to the pistachio tree), phlomis, and many more—all the low-growing aromatics. These plants combine interesting foliage color and strong, wind-resistant shapes that make billowing clumps, spreading masses. Indeed, they have all developed special techniques for dealing with long, hot, dry summers and flailing winds: thick, evergreen foliage to retain moisture (in the form of those famous, fragrant essences), green stems that continue the work of the leaves, gray "fur," thorns, or bulbous roots.

THE PROVENÇAL GARDEN

Clearly, the raw materials for making a garden in this region are tremendously varied, but not easy to use. People have learned to manage, generation by generation, since the beginning of time. And yet, many Provençaux deny that their region has any gardens! Some explain that this is a poor country where all efforts have traditionally been spent on survival. Nature here is certainly not exuberant, and gardens are always a form of oasis. But this is true of the Mediterranean world generally, Italy and Spain as much as Provence. The south of France, like these countries, has known many periods of prosperity and even luxury, when time and money were spent on pleasure and decor.

Others consider that Provence suffers from an "inferiority complex" with respect to northern norms, undervaluing its own traditions. It is also said that local reserve protects much-valued privacy. Or it may be a way of rejecting the cliché of the "paradise" image of Provence, and protesting against outside influences.

Above all, the problem is one of definition. Gardens today for most people mean English mixed borders. This wealth of summer color is the image usually proposed in the popular French garden press—although numerous British gardeners recognize the appeal of Provençal models to the point of attempting gray-leaved, aromatic "Mediterranean" gardens in their own climate.

Provence has always hung suspended between the Mediterranean and the north, shifting from Roman to Frankish domination, subject as of the fifteenth century to the French kings and then to the centralizing magnetism of Paris, while keeping its roots deep in Mediterranean soil, climate, and mores. The area has always been a meeting-place and a crossroads, and as such it occupies a situation almost unique in Europe. Even Roman influence was, after all, once foreign, though that graft took so well that all later growth stemmed from it. The seventeenth-century nymphaeas of Aiguebelle are said to be inspired by Roman triumphal arches —but Provençal, not Italian ones. In gardens, clearly, as with cuisine and language, shared features must often be attributed to common origins rather than to imitation of a foreign model.

It is evident, however, that Provençal gardens have never set trends for the rest of Europe (unlike, at times, southern poetry and painting). And where they imitate outside tastes (Italian, French or English), there is often a considerable time lag in the local applications. At its worst, such tardy inspiration can mean badly misunderstood, clumsily assimilated models that produce unbalanced mixtures. At its best, however, divergence from external dictates means an adaptation to Provençal needs and custom, to the "spirit of place." These gardens that were never in the forefront of fashion have thus retained a great variety, depending on whether they are sited in a village, around a farmhouse or a château, in the "pays d'Arles" or the Luberon, or on the outskirts of Aix-en-Provence.

The language comparison may be apt here once again. In spite of its fame in the late middle ages (when Dante nearly chose it for his *Divine Comedy*), southern French never became the language of a modern nation-state, used to

*Modern gardens feature plants with
strong Mediterranean connotations—particularly the olive and the cypress.
But lavender, here present in the
Cornwell garden, is not nearly as common as is generally imagined.*

convey a unified identity to outsiders. As a result, though it has retained enough cohesion to be called "Langue d'oc," "Occitan" or "Provençal," each area of the Midi has its own speech, easily mistakable for a country dialect. So it is with southern gardens. There is much divergence within general patterns, but none of the standardization that an appeal to an outside audience would have imposed.

The unity of this regional style comes inevitably from that same logic of land and climate, from those same forces that also determine farming practices and, for that matter, traditional rural architecture. The very "elements" that have been seen to shape the landscape—sun, water, et cetera—have also defined the character of Provençal gardens.

Sunshine in the garden means the famous Provençal light, which can be harsh at noon in high summer with shadows that are correspondingly deep and well defined. The fifteenth-century painting *School of Avignon* was celebrated

for just this dramatic, almost brutal contrast (so different from the subtle chiaroscuro practiced elsewhere). Some art historians argue that it prefigures the geometries of Cézanne and Picasso, similarly inspired by the sculpturing qualities of Mediterranean light. In this climate, the sun is a more active and less neutral partner than in a northern one, imposing constraints, demanding attention. At its best perhaps in late winter and early spring, when the mistral has produced this marvel that envelops you like a liquid, it gives as much pleasure, all by itself, as a whole garden of flowers.

Light (and sky) are thus not simply a backdrop here for a garden spectacle, but a living, changing, participating presence. The sun is never allowed unmitigated dominion in the garden, however. Southerners have learned to create many sorts of light and shade for different seasons and times of day, allowing for many color variations and changes—effects like backlighting can occur throughout the day. Color

*Southern custom carefully modulates sun and shade
for varied effects at different seasons. At the Jas Créma, a sheltered
stone bench will store the sun's heat in winter.*

and form are always modulated, negotiated, calculated. In summer, the hard brilliance of light is deflected, filtered or contained by a variety of shade-producing plantings, often layered with tall trees above, evergreen shrubs below outlined by a still lower, and darker, clipped hedge. This play of light throughout the day and year can be as important for the beauty of a garden as it is for a Cistercian church. Indeed, Provençal decors often echo Cistercian severity, similarly rejecting the elaborate, multicolored ornamentation of northern styles. Wonderful effects can be gained from the sober juxtaposition of a pale or golden wall and the deep texture of cypress, boxwood, laurustinus. Flowers are not absent, but command attention mainly as seasonal accent—wisteria, Judas trees, tamarisk, lagerstroemia and so on. Edith Wharton, in a comment that fits all Mediterranean gardens, put it very well: "It is hard to explain to the modern garden-lover, whose whole conception of the charm of gardens is formed of successive

pictures of flower-loveliness, how this effect of enchantment can be produced by anything so dull and monotonous as a mere combination of clipped greenery and stone-work. . . ."

"Clipped greenery" can be a major attraction in Provence, where the shaping of garden plants continues the practices of agricultural pruning. Few Provençal gardens exist without formal elements such as sculptured plants or stone, or both. This is neither the controlled domination familiar from the imposing château gardens of the north, nor the elaborate display of majestic southern villas, but an ordering that seeks harmony for both plant and planter. It produces the apple cordon, the grape arbor, and the knobby, umbrella-like planes that shade the house in summer. The darker evergreens (box, euonymus and yew) lend themselves to formal shaping, at the very least as hedging. Public roads climbing the wild slopes of the Luberon and the Alpilles, or in the Gard, at altitudes where box grows wild and plentiful,

Provençal gardens make the most of layered plantings that filter the strong southern light. The result can be marvelous backlighting effects, as here at the Vallon Raget.

are often bordered by such hedges, simply clipped into roundness by the machines of local maintenance teams in a manner unexpected outside a *jardin à la française*. But the inspiration is not French; it is too popular, too practical and too diverse.

Pushed as far as topiary, it can be quite fanciful. Indeed, popular Provençal topiary may well be a Roman vestige: the invention of tree-clipping is attributed by Cicero to G. Matius, who was active at the end of the first century B.C., when Roman influence in Provence was at its height. Circles, squares, disks and spheres now appear everywhere, seemingly an anomaly until one begins to realize how common they are. The entrance to a farm courtyard or access road will be flanked by elaborate plant sculptures; many simple gardens near farms or in villages contain one or two smaller layered shrubs; a farmstead near Saint-Etienne-du-Grès has a low, bell-shaped boxwood parterre among large shade trees. One of the best repositories (so to

speak) for the Provençal art of topiary is the cemeteries, where many small communities have traditionally expended their best garden efforts. Eyguières, Goult and Forcalquier offer famous sculptures, lovingly maintained. This is one compelling example of how Roman, French, Italian, and local influences can become inextricably intermingled.

The stone that so often stands in contrast to greenery is similarly carved and shaped, but usually paler than the vegetation (while in the north it is often darker). Stone in a Provençal garden means mass, light, texture, coolness, decor, form. It can determine temperature and luminosity. It often completely dominates the garden: as sculpture, as furniture, but also as walls that encircle and retain. Provençal gardens invariably involve layers and levels, whether on an entire hillside or in the patio of a village house. Inevitably, elaborate traditions of wall gardening have evolved.

Plant sculpture in Provence
ranges from the folk art of topiary, found in many village cemeteries,
to extremely sophisticated decors.
Is this the effect of French or Italian influence, or simply Provençal?

Walls hold in that precious and essential element, the earth, which wind and storms would so readily sweep away. Practical economy and regional style are here again inseparable. Provençal gardens are not the landscaping that comes after the architects have finished. They form a whole with the site and the buildings, themselves made from local materials according to century-old customs. Local earth gives color

to the washes that may cover the stone constructions, local clay provides roof tiles. The resulting harmony between habitat and landscape is one of the most beguiling charms of this countryside.

Water is life's blood for southern gardeners, who rarely seek to imitate its natural violence. Contrary to the great Italian examples, here there are few momentous cascades tumbling over hillsides, or elaborate leaping springs, facetious or decorative. Violent water has seemed the antithesis of the Provençal's efforts, not his inspiration; and in this once again he resembles more the frugal farmer than the extravagant prince.

Few gardeners forgo the pleasures of water's conspicuous ornamental presence, however. If sometimes it is flowing, and sometimes calm and reflective, it always emerges somewhere in the ideal synthesis of both: the fountain. No single feature of the Provençal landscape and garden complex is more venerated than this, whether

Dryset stone retaining walls are present
in almost every garden, as here in the abbey garden of Saint-André (top).
The formal gardens of the Chartreuse de Bonpas,
enclosed in medieval battlements, dominate an ancient river ford—now a major
traffic artery, and soon a route for the TGV train (above).

it gives life to a community or animates a private haven.

Modulations of sun and shade, textures of stone and earth—all this can be felt on the skin and breathed into the lungs. Provençal gardens are full of fragrance and country sounds (the nightingale's song, the cicada's hum), and touch (those thick, sticky or spiky leaves, the bark of a plane tree, the brush of foliage that releases its perfumes). And of course taste, the fruits of the garden. . . . Perhaps Provençal gardens have been overlooked because they are less dominantly visual than northern French ones? They indeed provide enchantment for all the senses, in all seasons.

DELIGHT AND PROFIT

The great gardens of the French tradition were usually the creation of a leisured elite that wished to distinguish its pleasures from practi-

cal pursuits and its gardens from the surrounding landscape. This phenomenon is rare in Provence. Here, on the contrary, the production of food has not been separated from aesthetic gratification. Similarly, time has not traditionally been divided into work and leisure, chores and fun; all through the long working day, it is still customary to "take time for living."

In sum, delight and profit intermingle. While for northerners, this interpenetration of the useful and the agreeable precludes a true garden tradition, it is just this tendency that creates Provence's best effects: vegetables, fruit, aromatics and flowers keep happy company, the shaded patio gives onto an orchard. Garden and rural landscape are not separate and opposing entities but parts of the same harmony. And today, of course, when decorative vegetable gardening appeals to an ever-larger public, Provençal models have much to offer.

To take but the simplest example: the trellis shading the southern façade of any traditional Provençal house. Dense, green summer foliage refreshes the eye, turning gloriously red and orange in autumn. Its winter branches form patterns on the stone, and their careful pruning adds the pleasure of a delicate job well done. Its climbing vine will often be seconded by wisteria, whose early spring blossoms lighten yet another season, while its leaves and golden fall color contrast perfectly with those of the vine. The latter gives of course the bounty of its grapes; both plants provide abundant summer shade but leaf out late enough to admit the winter sun. The wisteria flowers perfume the entire terrace, recurring off and on throughout the summer; but even the vine leaves smell good. This is a banal but typical example of a planting that appeals to all the senses, throughout the year.

Rome here again provided the model. In his book on Roman gardens, Pierre Grimal describes the primitive, sacred wood of a domestic sanctuary as a symbol of lost paradise. The latter, he explains, evoked a small farm garden where the owners could pick their own produce. This was a vision that united fruitfulness,

Provençal stonework has a language of its own, found in the unusual steps that link terraced levels and the detailing of its construction. It can be learned at the Conservatoire des Terrasses en Culture in Goult.

In the Provençal garden,
bright color may stand out at any time of year. Winter persimmons and
euonymous berries here keep company
with the equally brilliant autumn foliage of the Virginia creeper.

independence, and rural virtue, where even the vegetable garden was considered noble. Though by the beginning of the first century B.C. it had become something of a myth, Grimal estimates that examples could still be found on the outskirts of towns, among large domains transformed into parks, all through the days of empire. These rustic enclosures were called *hortuli* and traces of them appeared even in the pleasure gardens of Pompeii, where the peristyle of the house of Polybius contained fig and cherry trees, pears and a young olive tree, as well as various "low plantings." Their fruiting was so abundant that stakes were needed to hold up the branches.

The Roman dream of autonomy on one's own land persisted for two thousand years. In the fifteenth century Good King René, Count of Provence, granted a petition requesting the right of every landowner to refuse admittance to his own fields and orchards if he so desired. An eighteenth-century jurisconsult noted this judge-ment with approval and quoted "the old Provençal saying whereby a man is lord of his own land and of the fruits that grow therein." The Roman pastoral ideal was still, so to speak, bearing fruit; and even today southern farmers have a reputation for determined individualism.

Small peasant gardens are not a modern creation in the south. Van Gogh admired one for its "amazing color": "The dahlias are a rich and somber purple; the double row of flowers is rose and green on one side, and orange with hardly any leaves on the other. In the midst is a dwarf white dahlia, and a little pomegranate with flowers of the most vivid reddish-orange, with yellowish-green fruits, in the morning in full sunshine, in the evening drowned in shadow thrown by the fig trees and the reeds." Flowers, fruit trees and vegetables all intermingle.

Some traditional farm gardens occupy entire estates, which still sleep unsuspected near the most modern metropolises. This is true of a domain set around a large courtyard, facing

In 1888, Van Gogh noted peasant gardens that combined vegetables, fruit and flowers: roses and dahlias of many hues, figs and pomegranates. Provençal "kitchen" plots are still widespread, and are found even in the heart of elegant estates.

south, whose stately wrought-iron gate gives directly onto the family fields and orchards. The seventeenth-century façade has an old sundial and a trellis extending its full length, up which climb red and coral roses. The view from the upper-story windows of the courtyard below of the trellis, the urns planted with roses, the gate opposite and the fields, gives a sense of gentle enclosure. To the west is a smaller wrought-iron gate girded by neatly rounded boxwood hedging and behind this, a shrine with sculpted stone benches. Steps have been decorated with pots, out of which tumble cascades of flowers. There is a stone table with more benches in a sheltered corner, a pleasant area of summer shade and year-round fragrance. A shrub border leads past an iris garden, behind which is the henhouse—containing, typically, pheasants as well as chickens.

The owners of this property know every variation of weather and soil, but also all the

problems of international marketing. House and garden are inseparable here; so are elegance and agriculture. This is not the most elaborate of Provençal gardens, neither is it the most ancient nor the most modern, but it illustrates a kind of grassroots gracious living—unpretentious, attuned to the seasons and the earth. The charm of this stately property has not remained entirely obscure, however: a theater troupe chose this courtyard for its summer production of Chekhov's *Cherry Orchard*.

These are the most Provençal of gardens, those that their owners often disclaim as "not gardens at all." So insists Mlle. de T, a woman of old family who, in spite of war injuries, very competently runs a complex farm operation near Tarascon. The property was purchased by her father in the 1920s, when its income came largely from the surrounding vineyards. After the war, Mlle. T grew cherries and apples for a long time. For the the last ten years, however, she has converted much of the land to wheat, corn and sunflowers. She looks at a neighbor's field prepared for spring planting and mentions that the same land has already produced cabbages that were set out in October. Now, here it is, ready to go again with something else! Of course they work it themselves, she adds, that is what makes this possible.

Her estate has kept two large fragments of its original stone balustrade edging the large terrace. In front lies a stretch of lawn with mixed trees, a semi-oval space bordered by distant cypress hedges, leading toward a majestic lane of horse chestnuts that now vanishes

Many vegetables have decorative flowers such as the zucchini blossom, often eaten as fritters or stuffed (top); as well as artichokes and cardoons (above).

among the fields. At the point of juncture is a *gloriette* she calls the pheasant cage, planted with pale pink climbing roses. On the house itself (half farmstead, half château) climbs Virginia creeper, behind contrasting, clipped cypress and boxwood clumps. A small park area east and north has footpaths for shady walks, dense with maritime pines, laurustinus and untrimmed bay laurel. Near the house, laurel is carefully pruned at several different heights, providing dark shapes and masses that contrast with the filtered shade above and beyond. From the terrace, these plantings frame eastern fields and a view of the Alpilles beyond a line of plane trees. Last year, says Mlle. de T, that distant perspective was planted with sunflowers.

As we stood there in mid-March, while Mlle. de T insisted that her property was nothing more than a working farm, the fragrance of laurustinus was almost overpowering. Some of its flowers had been combined with wild plum branches (from the meadow hedge) to make a bouquet for the fireplace indoors. The grass was peppered with wild daisies, and acanthus foliage was already swelling in stately tufts along the edges of path, where the white crowns of wild garlic were gathering force. Nearby was a new planting of mixed white-flowered shrubs. The young foliage of the planes was luminous and warmly colored. Bordering the formal half-oval, a large cherry orchard of ancient trees was preparing to bloom, with the horse chestnuts following fast. In September, the woods would be yellow with sternbergia. Everywhere was a wide variety of outlines, volumes, paths, rhythms,

planned to create pleasure year round. The house itself was beautifully integrated into the landscape, protected from the wind but with good connections in the right places. But this, of course, is not really a garden. . . .

The Roman dream put down deep roots. Still today, the Provençal garden means delight and profit intermingled in the blessing of fertility. Fruit is as important as flower, because it is flower's fulfillment. This vision, these farming traditions, this hopeful human symbiosis with the violences of nature create small privileged spaces for growth. And today, all this provides inspiration for an infinite variety of new Provençal gardens.

Two examples of old Provençal domains in which architecture and plantings form an artful ensemble of great beauty . . . but are these gardens?

FRAMES
AND LINES

Garden design in Provence owes much to the intricate patternings of the rural landscape. The Provençal garden concentrates within itself the formal outlines and free flow of the countryside beyond; it is neither a welcome refuge in an alien desert, nor an ornamental park seeking to distinguish itself from humble surroundings, nor yet the reduction of the landscape to its simplest metaphysical components. Boundaries rarely isolate it from the landscape: each includes the other in a continuing reciprocity.

In her book *Green Architecture and the Agrarian Garden*, Barbara Stauffacher Solomon judges that "agrarian garden design constitutes an ideal synthesis between formal and picturesque traditions." She explains that "Western agrarians cultivated the land in simple geometric patterns. Rectangular fields were cut from the wilderness or marked by roads and rows of trees on the plains. Orchards were planted in orderly grids. Crops grew between straight furrows. The logic of the land and concern for cultivation determined patterns on the land. This work used planted materials with the same utilitarian logic and pride in performance needed in the traditional use of building materials; the result often was a landscape of collected splendor." She finds her best examples in Italy and California (and indeed the term "splendor" may be more appropriate for these regions than for Provence); but the French Mediterranean examples are simply less well known.

Such harmonious blending of form and flow reflects the choices made by different generations, successive populations, in dividing up the land. In Provence, natural divisions between valley land and hillside have imposed contrasting patterns: slopes were often painstakingly terraced with dry-set stone walls, while flatter land was cut into the typically southern patchwork we know today. It is possible to read in this countryside the layers of time and use that first created local lines and frames, and that now happily inspire modern garden design.

LAYERS IN THE LAY OF THE LAND

Terraced hillsides constitute one of the most characteristic Mediterranean landscapes. Certainly there is no more dramatic example of effective lines and framing than these giant hillside steps that so beautifully hug the contour of the slope even as they counteract its verticality. Their retaining walls, which permitted farmers to extend their holdings on land otherwise impossible to cultivate, provide sheltered spaces with incomparable opportunities for climbing and hanging plantations. For the person walk-ing along them, up or down the hill, they pro-vide an ever-varied sequence of spaces leading to discovery, while the viewer on the opposite side of the valley has a complete picture of their complex rhythms. Here lies an unusual and successful synthesis of formal and irregular elements, practicality and beauty, theme and variation.

Traces of terracing have been found in digs around Greco-Ligurian *oppida*, those earliest fortified hilltop settlements. When the Romans extended their vineyards, they discovered the advantageous microclimates of these sites for the ripening of grapes. Authorities disagree on the dating of the modern walls—the eleventh century, reconstructed in the fifteenth? Possibly built during the demographic pushes of the eighteenth and nineteenth centuries? All concur that they do not lend themselves easily to modern farming methods and machinery.

An association in Avignon called APARE, connected to the Ministère de l'Environnement, is trying to find practical solutions for their maintenance and rehabilitation. This group recently produced a fine volume called *Paysages de terrasses* (Edisud), which explores the facets of these landscapes in France and elsewhere in the world.

Curiously, the silver crags of the Alpilles between Avignon and Arles have never been reclaimed in this manner. Is it because the topsoil disappeared too completely, too soon? Or the slope was too steep, as on the upper reaches of the Dentelles de Montmirail? Perhaps early Roman occupation organized so thoroughly the

Hillsides of stone-walled terraces, characteristic of Mediterranean landscapes, create spectacular lines and rhythms, especially when filled with orchards in spring flower.

valley lands at their feet—the stony Crau as pasture for huge flocks of sheep, the northern plain as fertile, irrigable fields still highly productive today—that terracing was unnecessary. In any case, the triangular plain between Arles, Tarascon and Saint-Rémy, along with the Comtat Venaissin to the east, posses the richest bottom land of the area.

Provençal valleys characteristically offer a crazy quilt of small, irregular plots on which a great variety of crops are grown. These patterns also date back to the beginnings of agriculture. Early road lines were often determined by the biennial migration of Paleolithic flocks, while arable land was cut up and planted by the first Neolithic farmers. When the Romans arrived, summoned by the Greek trading community of Marseille, they settled in not as pioneers discovering virgin land but as reformers of an already shaped countryside.

Reform they did, however, with drastic

consequences. The valley landscapes that we see today were largely created by them. In his history of the French landscape, Jean-Robert Pitte states that Roman conquest of Gaul engendered for several centuries a homogenization of the landscape that was not seen again until the industrial revolution. Provence was subject to this influence two centuries longer than any other part of the country.

Julius Caesar initiated these rural reforms after the fall of Marseille. Tribal territories were regrouped around the new cities, obtaining different judicial status according to the loyalty of their owners. The whole countryside was surveyed and divided into "centuries"—a monumental undertaking. Besides aerial photographs, other evidence of this process exists: 415 marble fragments of the survey called the Cadastre d'Orange (visible in the museum of that town). It has been estimated that the limits of today's communes, the network of modern roads and even railroads still owe a heavy debt to this survey.

"Centuriation" created a grid pattern for the rural landscape comparable to that of the Roman city plan, and similar, perhaps, to the American townships, without covering the same vast spaces. Fields were divided into squares of about 35 meters along one side—a size surprisingly common even today. Roman law also gave equal shares of land to each son rather than the entire estate to the eldest, a practice that kept holdings small and eventually scattered them about the countryside in a manner that has made land reform particularly difficult in modern times.

Cypress hedging is a relatively recent feature of Provençal landscape: it was introduced only in the late nineteenth century, when newly spreading irrigation networks led many farmers to turn to intensive market gardening. New crops were sorely needed to replace olive orchards, which were destroyed in the terrible frosts of 1870, and considered a bad investment. So it was that many of Van Gogh's subjects were planted just in time for him to enjoy them in 1889.

The geometries of the Provençal landscape

Irrigation canals and hedging
create still other lines in the landscape. Bamboo (Arondo donax),
dried and used in the pliable fencing
known as canisse, *protects the bare feet of cypresses and poplars (above).*
The silver tones of the olive trees
contrast with the red and ocher hues of the countryside, as here
at the Fontaine-de-Vaucluse (opposite).

thus combine ancient and modern elements. Windbreaks and hedges, retaining walls, canals, and field divisions determined by Roman law frame the symmetries of the crops themselves, grown today in ever greater regularity to permit the use of modern equipment, but in fields of all shapes and sizes.

Southern fields appeal by their colorful variety, within which crops grow in neat, evenly spaced rows, orderly to the point of geometric perfection. The spectacle changes constantly throughout the seasons, but is perhaps most striking in autumn when each variety of fruit tree and vine takes on a different hue. Even when bare earth dominates, its colors vary greatly from one region to another. The *garrigue* is always there, foreground and background.

Asparagus, with its spring mounds covered in clear plastic, its summer plumes that stay deep green even in drought conditions and its brittle branches golden in autumn, occupies

large rectangular tracts of sandy soil often juxtaposed with vineyards, especially in the Gard. Sunflower fields visible from a great distance delight the traveler, art historian, farmer and gardener alike. More fragile crops are protected by giant cypresses that can make even orchards seem dwarfed in comparison. How piquant the contrast between that green-black fur and fat, shiny cabbage rows, or tiny red oak-leaf lettuce newly planted. . . .

FIELDS IN THE GARDEN

The frames and lines of agriculture have affected the modern Provençal garden in numerous ways. Terracing now provides sheltered sites for innovative ornamental plantings, giant rockeries; on flatter land, cypress-hedged compartments, established for vegetable crops, have been maintained as garden "rooms." Equally impressive is the incorporation, right in the heart of many contemporary designs, of rows of

Many modern Provençal gardens incorporate entire fields and orchards into their heart. The terraced domain of Princess B has kept its olive trees, protected by a dramatic cliff behind.

fields and orchards, making the land's original agricultural plan one of its main ornamental features.

It is easy to understand how this happened. When contemporary gardens are designed around former agricultural holdings, it is natural that some of their internal divisions should correspond to the original elements—wise, in fact, since the farmer's plan was certainly not arbitrary, but determined by the best growing conditions. It is similarly understandable that new owners of rural properties are often attracted by the compelling lines of drystone walls on a hillside, a dazzling lavender field in bloom, magnificent cypress hedging or ancient olive orchards, and wish to retain the features that inspired their initial purchase. The resulting retention of agricultural designs in the garden's very heart is a major characteristic of the neo-Provençal school, and one of its great originalities.

One striking terraced garden has been cre-

ated east of Avignon by Princess B. She is willing to undertake the labors involved in maintaining her stone walls—even when, as recently, a curved corner some four meters high fell down overnight in a storm. She has two essential advantages here: a local stonecutter familiar with the old techniques, and a pale, blond limestone that will allow recent work to blend almost imperceptibly with older building.

Once owned by the Sade family, her lordly farmstead lies under the crest of the hill in a particularly wild *garrigue* setting. The terraced part sits just below and above the house. Climbing roses and jasmine moving up the latter's west wall lead the eye up to the several layers beyond, above which more immense, jutting rocks dominate the landscape.

The house has adapted the horizontal forms of its surroundings. To the east lies a new garden installed on a succession of particularly narrow terraces. All along the back wall of the main level, a raised bed contains simple plantings

In the garden of Princess B,
the path leads up through natural outcroppings surrounded by copses of huge,
gnarled oaks. Small patches of rosemary,
thyme and clumps of Spanish broom are planted near fragments of ruins.

of cistus, dark blue ceanothus, euphorbias, and self-sown wild poppies; jasmine again climbs upward, meeting ivy falling from above. The stone columns of a long pergola stand on the level above, along with clusters of olive trees, almonds, and more broom.

This property is particularly well integrated into the landscape, very Provençal, a fine blend of simplicity and sophistication. Princess B has stressed both the transformation of rock into stone wall, and of hill into cultivated terrace. The result is a highly structured garden focused on a particularly refined house, whose elegant, beautifully planted patios, half indoors, half outdoors, surround an old well.

A different sort of terraced garden by the Rhône is situated on town heights once planted with fruit and olive trees. The slope is particularly steep, the view across the river stunning. The modern house faces onto a cleared flat space of lawn around a basin, surrounded by slanting pines and shrubberies, but the main garden lies

behind and above. A serpentine path leads through a dense mix of leveled plantations, some pruned into geometrical balls and cones, other left wild, in which olive trees, cistus, roses and iris create varied rhythms. This is a garden that displays a concern for texture and foliage, where color counts mainly as seasonal highlight, and the light is filtered and soft. A higher section is reached by a long set of stone steps, a vertical axis on the hillside. At their top lies the swimming pool, protected by steep walls along the back.

The retaining walls in the lower sections are almost hidden by the luxuriance of the vegetation, and certainly stone plays a much smaller part here than in the last garden. Where it does appear, however, it is most unusual, for it takes the form of the polished Rhône pebbles, contrasting on the lowest level with succulents (agaves and yuccas). The same pebbles have even been used to make an interesting, original fountain. As they also serve for the paving of the

In this mountain garden,
the long lines of a field of lavender entice and direct the visitor to a pool with
a gloriette at the end (top).
A clever blending of natural and wild elements creates strong garden character
in this terraced property in the Rhône valley (facing).

public lane outside the garden, they integrate the latter into its setting.

Dry mountain hillsides have been the traditional site for fields of lavender, the plant that is for many people a symbol of the Provençal garden. Most recently installed gardeners want at least a few plants and a whole field if they have room, as a vivid prospect for far or middle ground that will glow for a month or more, or turn geometrically gray or green according to time of year. Rocky soil and intense sun bring out its full fragrance and color.

Lavender was long a focal point in the garden of the Jas Créma, perhaps the most famous in Provence, owned and designed by the Baroness de Waldner. Here large fields provided a transition between the garden's heart and outlying plantations of olive and cherry orchards and vines. Set on the sort of hillside where all these things might grow for purely utilitarian reasons, this garden still links more deeply than any other, on this scale at least, agricultural geometries and garden formalities. The entire property is tended by the owner and one farmer-gardener, the assiduous Mr. Dos Santos; and there is a unity of feeling about garden and fields that comes from the same careful ordering and attention applied to both. The lavender made the connection explicit, since its rows were arranged as a formal parterre. Vertical accents came from arches decked principally with yellow banksia roses, contrasting beautifully with the soft tones of the plantings out of season. And when the fields flowered, a back wall richly clothed in golden Mermaid roses

added the right contrast to what became a flowing sea of lavender.

This part of the garden has now been completely dug up to allow for the planting of olive orchards in place of the lavender parterre—still outlined with formal rosemary hedges. Lavender will be planted once more around the olive canopies, and the combination still provides strong ties with the agricultural setting.

Decorative lavender fields are now often planted in the fertile bottom lands of valley gardens, where they may suffer from having their feet in the water. Nonetheless, a large swath may provide a dramatic central feature, as in couturier Bernard Perris's garden near Eygalières. This vast rectangle is enclosed in tall, dense cypress hedges on the north and south sides, their lines repeated by rows of vines. Beds of modern roses were added northeast and perennials for cutting northwest, underplanted with cerastium. The southern edging includes, besides the vines, a row of small laurel and boxwood cones, spikes, and topiary balls on sticks. All this serves as a frame for the lavender. At the far east end of this long rectangle, surrounded by rose hedges and covered with Virginia creeper, is the platform containing the raised swimming pool.

Mr. Perris's garden was originally designed by English landscaper David Graham. Besides its inclusion of a lavender field in its very heart, it makes the most of another equally striking feature of farming heritage: the entire two-acre property has been created out of three rectangular, cypress-hedged vegetable fields running

*Lavender parterres
in the famous Jas Créma garden have now been planted with ancient olive trees,
but the arches of banksia roses and clematis remain (top).
Lavender provides the background for the topiary towers and Nozomi roses,
trained on arches, in the Jas Créma garden (above).*

(as is customary) east-west. The cypresses are now clipped, and wide openings have been made directly in front of the house to allow a perspective down to the last row. Thus three distinct compartments, meant to protect the fragile produce of a market garden, have been maintained as garden "rooms."

The "Provençal" lavender garden occupies the central and most important of the three. In the first, next to the road, lies the farmstead itself. Each end of its rectangle combines ornamental and food plants: there is a small vegetable garden to the east, beyond a flower-decked well, and to the west, a mixture of fruit and ornamental shrubs. Gooseberry bushes and peonies form a hedge and mark a slight change of level. In the third "room," the one beyond the lavender garden, one discovers to the east a collection of weeping trees around a teak bench; the west end has a formal rose garden hedged with cherry laurel. At the extreme west is an unexpected space: a small, flower-

edged plot for playing occasional *boules* games.

The "rooms" of this garden, unlike their English counterparts, have retained a larger scale, a strong sense of orientation with respect to climate, and the simplicity of agricultural plantings. Much elegant detail has been added— and 1,700 roses!—but there is not the density of planting of a collector's garden. The term "Provençal garden" may not be appropriate if meant to evoke the traditional gardens of old farmsteads, but can very well serve to acknowledge the rural inspiration of this highly decorative domain.

Another garden on the fertile plains north of the Alpilles has also kept its cypress hedging, but this time there are five separate spaces. Directly in front of the *mas*, one hedge has been removed where the land slopes gradually up from the house. The lawn here has been graded into a series of very low terraces, each held by a stone step extending the length of the field. These differences of level are accentuated by the placing

In the garden of Bernard Perris,
a swath of brilliant lavender shines between the cypress hedging originally
planted to shelter spring vegetables.

of old pots full of geraniums, unusual sculpture (such as a Hungarian baptismal font), and distant tree groupings (olive trees in particular, though these owners are trying to succeed with dogwoods as well). From the house, the view is broken by one of the remaining cypress hedges. Yet this is a false limit: a small opening leads beyond to the swimming pool that occupies the farthest compartment, thus nicely secluded and out of sight.

The other three divisions lie to the north of the house, which was at one point a coach halt, so that its buildings extend not only in the usual east-west line but also north-south. The closest cypress hedge has been replaced by lower cherry laurel, though its lack is sometimes felt on days of mistral, in spite of the ivy and creeping vines planted for additional insulation on the house walls.

The final two compartments have remained somewhat wilder. The first field (still enclosed by hedging) is mown but unwatered grassland,

with roses along one end and raspberries on the other, both planted in formal array. It is cut in two by an original feature: a sheltered walk composed of various kinds of fruit trees, including olives, united by a simple border of chrysanthemums at their feet. This is a particularly delightful example of "edible landscaping."

The fruit trees included in this garden have become one of its most successful features. Entire orchards are now commonly found in the garden's heart—cherry, apricot or, most frequent of all, olive plantations. Few trees offer such a rich blend of decorative and utilitarian blessings as the olive. They readily combine into orchard symmetries, yet each one retains an unusual degree of individual personality.

In the Vallon Raget garden near Tarascon, the owners have kept an old olive plantation as the central feature of a complex modern garden, set on the hillside that rises in front of their family farmstead. Enormous and ancient trees (an Aleppo pine, a hackberry, *Robinia*

This garden in the Alpilles
is graced with spreading canopies of shade trees near the house,
a typical feature of the Provençal mas.

pseudoacacia and two cypresses) shade the house terrace facing this slope. It is held in by a low retaining wall supporting swaths of floral plantings (ceratostigma and salvias, lespedeza, centranthus and fragrant pelargoniums, with fuchsias and white nicotiana, among many others, in the shaded parts). The olive orchard is so close by, held in by the same low wall, that one row of trees has had to be removed. It is thus slightly above the house terrace—an unusual position. In fact, the property lies just at the foot of the northern side of the Alpilles mountains, while the farmstead, like all Provençal houses, faces south. The backlighting that appears through the silver foliage is one of this garden's finest effects.

This orchard is also clearly visible from other angles, including levels still farther above (the wilder reaches of the garden, blending rosemary, kermes oak, junipers and brooms of the local *garrigue*). Seen on the contrary from the western driveway, it is encircled by more low retaining walls: one supports a row of vines underplanted with cineraria, another has fountains of lespedeza. The statuesque olive trees are thus set into a new ornamental context by their colorful edgings, but also by climbing roses cascading over old branches.

Less immediately visible on first arrival is another "working" olive orchard, beyond the first and farther back, where plowed strips alternate with rough grass. Its retaining wall spills over with pink dwarf dahlias among huge bouquets of intense blue perovskia, stunning in the mid-summer sun.

This is a garden with much densely planted floral color. It contains many segments: a rose parterre, a shade garden around an old well with hostas, fuchsias and cotoneasters; a cypress arch supporting large-flowered clematis, a miniature cactus garden, an aromatic plot with knotted santolinas, a formal basin with water plants, a cascading spring from the hills above. But the olive orchard remains

*The Vallon Raget garden has several
distinct areas, including a shade garden hidden behind cypress hedging (above).
In its heart stands an ancient olive orchard,
slightly raised above the house terrace and visible from all sides (following double page).*

its dominant feature, sheltered by the fine old *mas* itself, in keeping with the latter's farm character.

Olive trees at the Vallon Raget, as in many other gardens, are today planted in lawns maintained by automatic watering. This new context for ancient trees raises many questions about the mixing of farm and garden and even, for some observers, about northern and southern models. When fields of agricultural origin are preserved in the garden, must they be cultivated as they always have been? The Vallon Raget has both types of olive orchard, of course, and its owners take as good care of their olive crop as of their flowers. But a similar olive plantation in the Val Joanis garden, north of Aix, is so well-watered that some trees have fallen sick as a result. Purists protest against any use of the sacred tree for ornamental purposes, even when not underplanted with lawn. And yet, so many imposing old orchards are being torn up that it is surely a homage to tradition to save them, even for garden use? Luckily these evocative, dramatic trees transplant easily even at an advanced age—they symbolize eternity, after all. So it is that even public authorities are setting out instant antiquity: three five-hundred-year-old olive trees appeared a few years ago on the east end of the Pont du Gard, and have prospered in spite of drought.

Orchards that are meant to produce fruit and oil should be plowed and fertilized, of course, but as the owner of another restored farmstead near Mouriès points out, this can be impractical because of the lack of access for machinery through the garden, and the difficulties of walking in the orchard afterward, especially in wet weather. She is lucky to have as a natural ground cover a wild aromatic savory (the famous "donkey pepper"), which she hopes will colonize her orchard. Up until now, it has been worked regularly. Many other attractive solutions have been found: a carpet of low-grow-ing hypericum, or, as at the Jas Créma, rings of iris far enough from the trunks to allow for annual feeding. The olive tree dilemma is a typical problem confronting modern gardeners who want to maintain ties with tradition, while being open to decorative innovation.

PATHS AND PASSAGES

The line that most immediately links the Provençal garden to the agrarian landscape is its access road. In larger properties this is often an impressive avenue of deciduous trees—planes usually, less often horse chestnuts or lindens—that prolongs the lanes sheltering southern highways. The latter were first begun in modern times by Renaissance monarchs who were not concerned with the Mediterranean climate but in need of wood for the gun carriages of cannons, ship masts, rifle butts, furniture and even matches. Whether public or private, these avenues afford protection from the fierce summer sun, creating soft, filtered light and a sense of protective enclosure, producing a pleasurable effect of magic passage in contrast to the glaring open spaces on either side. Their length may also impress the visitor with the extent of the owner's dominions. . . .

The transition from public road to private lane is often marked by two stone pillars, sometimes flanked by a small, sloping wall on either side. Some retain a wrought-iron gate that may bear the owner's coat of arms. Traditionally, only the eighteenth and nineteenth-century properties near cities like Aix and Marseille were enclosed in high walls, so that elsewhere the gate was more of a symbol than a barrier. Monasteries and old fortified castles were exceptions, of course, and often have long

Numerous private gardeners willing to spend small fortunes have recently added a row or even an entire orchard of enormous olive trees, which can be transplanted even when very old. Needless to say, a brisk luxury market is fast developing (above and opposite).

approaches inside the protecting walls. Such a long, enclosed lane may pass through one (or more) heavy, thick-walled arches that provide a cool and shaded transition to the open area within. The Chartreuse de Bonpas near Avignon has such an entrance. The contrast between dark passage and the sunlit space beyond is enhanced by the more common one between pale stone and dark vegetation. The traditional

reception terrace with its pots, fountains and shade trees becomes, in such a site, a courtyard enclosed in high walls: so it is also in the castles of Fontarèches and Issarts.

At the opposite extreme from such enclosure is the massive, dramatic ramp leading to the castle of Ansouis from the valley below (though visitors should arrive through the village). Starting from the typical gate pillars, it makes several sharp angles in its climb to the top, accented by tall cypresses as it mounts, with the fortifications soaring above. Vauban is said to have designed this, though there is apparently no proof, and the late Duchess herself was inclined to think it medieval. This road also makes a fine line on the landscape when seen from the castle; at its foot, near the lowest turn, is a Romanesque chapel with another much smaller zigzag access ramp, repeating the rhythm. The Roman-Renaissance garden on the lowest level, clearly visible from the castle, is planted around a rectangular pool, connected by a

Olive and other trees are underplanted
with a variety of ground covers, including hypericum and iris (above).
Avenues of majestic plane trees
generally lead to a Provençal château, but this one at the Château de Roussan
veers right at the last minute
and arrives at the sixteenth-century farmyard (opposite).

dens, paths and steps are important in delineating the composition but remain in themselves discreet.

The one exception is the shaded summer walk. The larger the domain, the more elaborate this is, the most ambitious creating lines so complex that they form a labyrinth. In some cases these become the classic French parterre, a large, open space whose patterns are clearest from the reception rooms of the house above (La Gaude, near Aix, is the most famous example). More typically in Provence, however, as at Fontarèches and Castille, shade trees are layered over the lower design, so that its lines must emerge from within. Once again, the Provençal version is graceful, even playful, rather than intimidating. It affords pleasure not only to the eyes, but also to the nose; to the ears, by the birds and insects it shelters; and even the skin, in its cool summer air.

Such shaded walkways are among the Provençal garden's most typical features, even without a parterre: plots of green oaks, box and laurustinus formally pruned near the house, left wild further away, are crisscrossed by several lanes that suddenly open onto the fields beyond. Numerous old domains, even small ones, have such gardens—one now shelters an archery range at its outer reaches.

There exists an even more characteristic version of the shaded lane: the *tèse*, in general use in the bastides of Aix and Marseille, but found also (though not always by that name) in country villas near other cities. A long stretch of shrubbery was planted on either side of the path to meet above the heads of walkers. Its function was not only to provide for cool promenades but to draw game for hunters. It allowed the leisured summer residents a combination of country pleasures: you could stroll in the shade and catch part of your dinner at the same time. Traditional gardeners kept an eye on migration routes to know just where a *tèse* would be most productive. These gentlemanly entertainments rarely contribute to the satisfaction of gardeners today, who more usually view hunters with misgivings. They are however characteristic of a culture that inevitably combines pleasure

canal to a smaller, pentagonal basin (box-edged, like the canal, for clear viewing from the summit above). The whole is a complex series of lines and forms that is thought to have been inspired by Bramante.

Inside the Provençal garden, paths are rarely a striking feature in their own right. Low hedges of santolina, box or lavender may make formal outlines close to the house. Stone slabs and low walls also emphasize transitions while supporting plants at the same time, often allowing closer viewing. Steps are almost always made of stone. Sometimes these can be monumental, however, the garden's central feature: thus the Jardin de la Fontaine in Nîmes, where eighteenth-century architects so valued their rococo lineage that they buried a Roman theater under a hillside to get their best effects. But this is rare, luckily, and belongs to public plantings or castle gardens in which authority and majesty are foremost. In most Provençal gar-

A typical stone entrance pillar, outside the Chartreuse de Bonpas.
Sculpted columns like this one mark the formal entrance to Provençal domains (above).
The charming garden lane of Saint-Paul-de-Mausole, once a monastery,
later Van Gogh's hospital refuge, is simply planted with hollyhocks, wisteria,
oleanders, acanthus and the inevitable box and laurustinus topiary (opposite).
The Roman reservoir at the
Château d'Ansouis is now used as a swimming pool (following page).

clematis has been planted at the foot of each pillar, with dwarf pittosporum providing the necessary protection at the roots, its clumps adding punctuation that accentuates the sequence. From this spot one can see the largest of the formal water gardens below. More traditional pergolas can be found at the Prieuré hotel and the Saint-André abbey gardens in Villeneuve, at the Pavillon de Bidaine near Aix, and in many other gardens.

HOUSE AND GARDEN

Describing Italian villa gardens, Edith Wharton noted that "terraces and formal gardens adjoined the house, the ilex or laurel walks beyond were clipped into shape to effect a transition between the straight lines of masonry and the untrimmed growth of the woodland to which they led, and each step away from architecture was a nearer approach to nature." Many Provençal gardens today observe this progression, though the final stage is more likely to be open fields, orchards or scrub than woodland. In the traditional plan, a paved terrace outlined by a clipped evergreen hedge or stone wall lies directly in front of the house on its southern side. (In more stately properties, the separation becomes a stone balustrade, giving onto a formal parterre.) Immediate transitions are usually carefully pruned evergreens, leading to more asymmetrical plantings (either flowers, shrubs or shaded walks, or some combination, according to style). An outlying area (still in the garden) is either agricultural or wilder in character, finally emerging on, blending with or including the surrounding landscape. Today space must often be found as well for a secluded parking lot, swimming pool and tennis court, none of which must be visible from the house directly, but all of which must be easily accessible without going through torrid sun. There is usually also some sort of service area and often the residence of a caretaker (recalling the house of the tenant farmer in a traditional domain whose owners, city dwellers, resided there mainly in the heat of the summer).

and practicality. Good examples still exist at the Domaine d'Albertas and the Château de la Gaude, near Aix.

Pergolas, at once more open and more formal than the shrubbery walkway, are less common. When they occur in this part of Provence, they rarely cut across hillsides, but make a dramatic vertical axis, as in some Riviera gardens. Usually they are constructed against the back retaining wall of a terrace, sometimes for more than a hundred meters. Their traditional elements are simple stone pillars, from which wires support the vines, wisteria and roses that usually cover them. Interestingly, the pergola is often situated higher than the main section of the garden, so that it serves not only as a connecting passage but as a viewpoint as well.

One such construction has been restored in château gardens near Tarascon, its floral roof enriched with trumpet vine and honeysuckle spilling over the wall above. A different sort of

Such a gentle movement from geometry to

Many Provençal châteaux have low, formal,
patterned hedging not intended for viewing from above but for shaded walking.
As in this famous tèse at Albertas, hunting small game was common practice (above).
The particularly elegant pergola of the Saint-André abbey
extends along the wall behind the rose parterre. The white doves that lodge
behind it can often been seen circling above the snowy banksia roses.
Iris and Sedum spectabile at its feet provide color in different seasons (opposite).

freer forms may imply that the house occupies a central position with respect to the garden; is visible from all its parts (as is often true for the "bastide" manor houses near Aix, set on top of a hillside); and that its windows give onto the garden, so that even the formal part close at hand can be viewed from above. The opposite plan to this is the "gate-way" design found on the Côte d'Azur, where the house (no matter how special its immediate surroundings), is simply a passage, soon out of sight in the large garden beyond. Neither of these garden designs dominates in the Rhône valley, but a combination is extremely common. In this plan, visitors arrive from the side (east or west) and are received in the sheltered southern courtyard or paved terrace in front of the house. The garden lies off to one side of the arrival point, and may have paths that lead up or down hill (or both). The house may then indeed be lost from sight momentarily because of differences of level or winding paths; it does not dominate the garden

but draws it together, acting as the point of convergence and the unifying focal point. Almost all lower Rhône valley gardens that have enough land to allow the choice have this layout.

The farmstead acquired in 1879 by entomologist Henri Fabre, on the edge of Sérignan-du-Comtat north of Orange, provides a good example: the internal access road approaches the house from the west side while the botanical and aromatic garden (formerly *garrigue*) extends in front, to the south. A low wall still separates the house terrace, with its traditional well, from the garden, reached though a narrow gate. Planting beds make formal patterns in the first reaches, getting wilder and wilder beyond. The house remains the central focus, but does disappear from sight at times, recurring here and there from a different angle. This is not a large garden, but a typical one, in spite of the unusual circumstances of its creation.

It is easy to think of some good reasons for

In a typical Provençal garden,
the house is a focal point but not the center. It does not dominate,
and may even be lost from view.

this pattern, but harder to know its exact history and distribution. Where wind protection from the north plays such a major role, designers must always have been loath to cut a hole in a north-facing hedge or wall for a driveway. The southern space, on the other hand, is precious for its shelter and must be reserved for more important things than transitions: the private family or formal reception area of the terrace, then the outlying garden, fields or orchards to be walked in and worked in. Whatever the causes, the effect is to create garden plans that do not intimidate the visitor by displaying from far off a grand façade or a breadth of plantations (this would also mean far too much exposure to sun and wind). The connection between human habitation, surrounding cultivation and outside landscape (wild or agricultural) remains loose, unforced, asymmetrical. There may well be surprises as the road curves round, and the view on arrival may be planned carefully for effect, but the unfolding achieves a pleasant and comfortable intimacy rather than majesty.

So it is that the traditional Provençal garden extends outward in an open manner, without the distinctly separate, hedge-enclosed "garden rooms" popular in its English counterpart. Frequently the topography suffices to create natural, internal distinctions—few indeed are Provençal gardens without differences of level.

Traditionally oriented south or southeast,
southern dwellings make the most of the protected space just in front—
a broad terrace shaded in summer, open in winter,
and the heart of family activities. As the greatest abundance of bloom
occurs here, it is also the heart of the garden.

Their designers rarely if ever find themselves with a large flat space to cut up as they please. Water distribution, extreme differences of soil quality in hill and valley, terraced hillsides and steep inclines can all impose an organization at the outset. Each part is closely linked to seasonal needs: there must be a shaded area in summer, a sunny but sheltered nook for the numerous fine December days. Water is organized for display but also for irrigation in times of drought. A viewpoint on the outside frames the growth, ripening and decline of the crops beyond. Of course the hedges may be removed, land leveled, water piped underground: but this produces suburban housing with little local character rather than a successful southern garden.

Two properties in Provence combine within themselves all the foregoing elements of garden design, created gradually over several centuries. The Saint-André abbey garden sits on a summit in Villeneuve, surveying neigh-

boring Avignon from the height of its fortified terraces, while the Château de Roussan, now a hotel, lies in the fertile plain north of the Alpilles off the road between Saint-Rémy and Tarascon. The first is a hillside construction with little topsoil and the dominating presence of stone; the second is very much a valley property, set among fields and irrigation canals. Both are well known and much loved by local populations, who accept them, with all their idiosyncrasies, as authentically Provençal.

The rocky peak of Saint-André in Villeneuve housed first a saintly sixth-century hermit, then a shrine, later a Benedictine abbey. The town that grew up around the latter was fortified during the Hundred Years War, and the abbey nestles within these ramparts, surrounded by its own high stone walls, like the germ in the heart of a seed. It is private property today, belonging to Mademoiselle Roseline Bacou, former curator of the Cabinet des Dessins at the Louvre. The public comes in discreetly for Sunday

*The rose parterre at Saint-André
was recently commended by the Inventaire National des Jardins as an exceptional
work from the early 1920s.
Rococo stone basins with benches protected by Judas trees, oleanders and
viburnum provide high focal points at each end.*

promenades; indeed local couples often go there for their wedding pictures, so that Mlle. Bacou finds her garden displayed in homes all over the area.

The abbey's main buildings were torn down at the time of the Revolution but one imposing house remains (of Romanesque, seventeenth and eighteenth-century construction). Sold in the early nineteenth century, it subsequently belonged to a lunatic who built an observatory to see the Island of Elba, to a convent, and finally to a distinguished art restorer and connoisseur whose friend, Emile Bernard, did a set of frescoes in one room. The garden was redesigned by two women of imagination in the 1920s, Elsa Koeberlé and a Russian artist friend, Genia Lioubov, who were familiar with the best talents of the time (Paul Claudel stayed here when visiting his sister in the asylum of Montfavet).

Visitors enter through a fortified gate and from the west side approach a broad public space in front of the main building. Large shade trees and an elegant, eighteenth-century arched wall (framing stone benches and statues) stand opposite the house itself, enclosing and inviting. The heart of the garden lies beyond, however: this is a formal rose parterre, edged with gray santolinas and organized in fan shapes. Statuary and two rococo stone basins with benches, protected by Judas trees, oleanders and viburnum, provide higher focal points at each end. Interestingly, this area was designed to be viewed from above, where the main buildings once stood, and whence a terrace still allows visitors to look down. The original neoclassical symmetry has been foiled by history and aided by perceptive garden planners, who realized that these irregularities are not foreign to the spirit of place.

Along the south side of this impressive central space stands a tall, double hedge of cypresses (a connecting path runs between). Beyond it lie narrow terraces on a lower level,

The two ruined churches
of Saint-Martin and Saint-André, complete with sarcophagi, are protected by
cypresses and pines and banked
with wild coronilla that is stunning in April.

planted with a mixture of roses, coronillas, Judas trees, iris, spiraea, Japanese quince, sedums and other local, even wild plants. These contrast with evergreens, pittosporums and box shaped into rounded domes. This more intimate and informally grouped shrubbery, surrounding statues of modest scale, provides a foreground for the fine views of Avignon across the river as well as wind protection for the viewer. One can lean over the wall to see very narrow spaces still farther below, somewhat abandoned now but with box-edged rectangles and fruit trees mixed together. The crenellations of the fortress walls provide another rhythm—this is, after all, a citadel. A whole series of these lower reaches (both those one can walk through and those one can only look down on) curves round the south and east sides of the garden, contrasting with the formality of the parterre in the garden's center.

This spectacular use of terracing differs of

course from both the rural and the Riviera hillsides in that only two levels, so far, are accessible: the lowest ones, though encircled by battlements, are too steep to be used as promenades from the house. One can, however, move upward. To do so means going through a passage so special, so magic that one feels like Dante accompanied by Virgil. The path takes one under fine, flat stone vaults, built to support both the weight of the house that used to be above and the cannons that stood guard in front of it. These vaults are so dramatic that Mlle. Bacou has chosen to restore them in preference to the house itself.

From under their protection, a narrow path winds upward between high walls, with bands of hypericum and ceratostigma at their feet. In this garden famous for its splendid views on all sides, one is momentarily enclosed, directed toward an unknown goal. Emerging on the upper level, one discovers the promenade overlooking the parterre, close once more to the house and the garden's center, protected by a row of old parasol pines laid flat on their side by the force of the north wind.

Still further above extends a hillside with a number of distinct areas. To the east stand the two ruined churches of Saint-Martin and Saint-André. Above, a gentle but compelling slope leads along an iris-edged path with cypresses at regular intervals, separating two large olive orchards standing in rough grass. These trees were mentioned in documents from 1803, and the eldest is judged to be some four hundred years old. At the highest point of the garden is a Romanesque chapel, the shrine of Saint Casarie, with more cypresses. These in fact structure the garden on all its levels and in all its parts.

The rest of the garden is a series of ruins from the original abbey buildings turned into garden spaces that mix formal settings and ever wilder shrubberies. One paved area is focused on an ancient Anduze vase on a pedestal amid olive trees, and a pattern of green and silver santolinas. This is called the fire garden because it is so protected from the mistral that bonfires can be safely lit here. It is now being

Roses can usually be found somewhere in a Provençal garden, whether they are carefully collected older varieties (some of which originated here) or the modern hybrids found at Saint-André (above). The santolina parterres of Saint-André in an unusual winter scene. Even in this season, the evergreen foliage, sculpture and strong lines of southern gardens maintain their beauty (opposite).

planted with various new shrubs and perennials.

The site is magnificent, the spaces intriguing. Mlle. Bacou plans to create greater texture and density, framing and connecting garden sections more clearly. Already in its present state the Saint-André garden is a kind of sourcebook of Provençal tradition—all the essential ingredients are here. But several possibilities present themselves for its restoration. Mlle. Bacou has received much expert but contradictory advice. Purists would have her remove all flowers, including the rose beds dating from the 1920s (which for the moment she has filled with Russian sage to prolong their flowering season). Others would have her, on the contrary, multiply the varieties, putting clematis in the olive trees, for example. The late Vicomte de Noailles advised her on color, suggesting that grays, pale pinks, violets, blues and pale yellows are most appropriate for the light and stone of this garden. He suggested working with the gray tones set by these elements, and avoiding too many flowers. Would he have appreciated the red-leaved berberis and cotoneasters now chosen for some of the wilder corners? Interestingly, southern visitors love this garden just as it is, whereas some English gardeners view it as an impressive stage yet to be peopled by its actors. There are many spaces with only one access (often just viewed from above), which could be made even more mysterious and inviting by appropriate plantings. However that may be, its design happily blends the surprises of topography with the whims of history; its plantations nicely combine a wide range of wild plants with others of garden and farm inspiration. The olive orchards are certainly one of the best features here. Paths and passages, connecting ruins from many epochs, are used to excellent dramatic effect. The house presides, welcoming, not dominating. The garden is enclosed and protected from that wicked wind, yet wide open at the same time.

The Château de Roussan may seem a totally opposite sort of property at first glance, but its designs have some similar elements, equally traditional. It provides an even more specific example of neoclassical inspiration accommodated to local custom and taste. Its layers of history also sit upon it lightly, at peace with each other in spite of potential incongruities.

The fifteenth-century farmyard still stands west of the main château buildings. The estate was ennobled after Roussan became the property of the Nostradamus family in the sixteenth century. The château itself is a creation of the late seventeenth or early eighteenth century. Its northern access road approaches with seemly symmetry, aiming at the middle of the elegant façade. At the last minute, however, it deviates, veering right to reach house and garden through the farmyard.

This avenue is lined with majestic plane trees (there are more than one hundred of these on the grounds, some three hundred years old). At its end, the house has been carefully placed to benefit from the best of seasonal extremes. The northern reception terrace, welcome in summer, is less intimate than the southern façade with its sundial that reads *Horas non numero misi serenas* (I count no hours but the sunlit ones). The middle "R" is writ large, for Roussan. The stone here comes from the nearby quarry of Les Baux-de-Provence, pale but flecked with green and gold.

From the middle balcony, one looks down onto the garden's main axis, which was designed to face the highest peak of the Alpilles in the distance, and is best seen from the upper story. Between this distant prospect and the garden area lie cultivated fields, once part of the park. Now farmed out, they are still considered decorative, and some summers are planted with sunflowers. Sometimes sheep pass in the distance.

The rest of the garden breaks comfortably with classical canons, blurring these careful symmetries with an art, and an artlessness, that combine for charming pastoral effect. To the south is a spectacular water feature, just visible from the house but to one side of the garden's main walkway. This is a stone Roman basin, with seventeenth-century sculpted figures. They suffered seriously during the war, losing their heads in fact (since recovered). The owner has identified them as goddesses, because of their special properties: Juno is big-breasted, Venus

At the Château de Roussan,
a pair of twin pillars draped with wisteria, flanked by two low walls,
purple plums and variegated ivy, define
the house terrace to the south—an idyllic spot for breakfast (opposite).
The rococo goddesses of this charming
Roman basin keep watch on the southern façade of the château
across the garden (following page).

carries Cupid, Diana stands with arrows and dog. The water piping is also Roman, running from the ancient, magic spring of Glanum to Saint-Rémy. Planned for extensive agricultural irrigation, now deteriorated, it is still efficient enough to supply this and several other properties in the area. There are stone canals bordering paths all through this garden and their flow provides a gentle murmuring, as well as connecting lines.

Water infuses the whole park from these conduits, which are no longer in perfect condition. Beside the pool rises a grove of young bamboo through which you can walk, peeking out at the garden from various angles. Larger bamboo (*Phyllostachys pubescens*) form a screen of thick gray and green stalks nearer the house. The nineteenth-century owners of this garden may have known Eugene Mazel, who created the impressive bamboo garden at Prafrance farther west with a passion that unfortunately bankrupt him. Many château gardens in the area benefited from it, however.

From the same period dates a well-proportioned greenhouse, set again, somewhat arbitrarily, off to one side, its iron superstructure supported by low stone walls like those outlining the garden's major areas (often with sculptured detailing).

This park has an untended air that subtracts not at all from its charm. There are roses everywhere, sometimes grouped into beds, sometimes climbing through a cypress. The grass grows tall, but there are deck chairs discreetly placed under trees. A pleasant feeling of comfort rather than grandeur comes from the absence of a definite, all-embracing angle of vision; one moves from one area to the next, looking each time at the rest of the garden from a fresh perspective. The house is always present, close by, reassuring even if occasionally lost from view. Some shrubbery is pruned, rounded, including the two purple plums near the entrance; box, even cypresses are deliberately

*The canal at Roussan runs discreetly
east-west behind a low gate, spreading to encircle a small island.
Its cool shade evokes Normandy more than Provence.*

top-heavy, and lagerstroemias punctuate every-where for late summer color. Others are left free: pomegranates, catalpas, even sequoias, and a lovely two-hundred-year-old persimmon tree with hanging, oriental-looking black branches, resplendent in autumn with golden fruit. There is beauty in the accents of color at all times of year, without a single moment of massive display.

These two properties, one perched on a hill-top, the other nestled in a valley, bring out the range of traditional Provençal garden design, the frames and lines that link such gardens to their settings and determine their interior divisions. And although one was for centuries a powerful abbey, and the other an elegant châ-teau, both have undergone the strong influence of agrarian inspiration. Today, however, the broadest scope for garden innovation is being provided not by impressive historical vestiges of this sort but by humbler domains: old farm-stead and village plots.

A well-proportioned, nineteenth-century
greenhouse is set apart so that its impressive structure
takes the stroller by surprise.
It is one of the garden's most intriguing features.

FARM AND VILLAGE

arly historians (Julius Caesar among them) already recognized two types of rural habitat in Provence: the valley farm and the hilltown house. Land was worked, crops produced, from these two bases, and the fruitful activities of Provençal country life revolved around them. The isolated farmsteads generally lay on fertile lowlands; their horizontal, spreading dwellings might house a single family of sharecroppers or an entire, self-sustaining community of people and animals, all governed by a patriarch. Their rectangular buildings were infinitely adaptable to diverse rural activities: viticulture, polyculture, truck farming, wheat growing, livestock raising, and an ingenious range of cottage industries. Villagers, in contrast, lived vertically: in small, high dwellings with room for only a few animals on the ground floor. The scattered bits of land they worked were situated on dry, stony slopes. Their tools were portable, their crops small: olives could be collected in a basket. The village community was also self-sufficient, but composed of poor farmers and day workers as well as specialized craftsmen who had a bit of land to work.

Mountain and valley shared the seasonal rhythms of production from the land. At its best, in times of plenty, this meant a rich and even elegant existence that has often been idealized since. From it has evolved a vision of pastoral perfection that still haunts both natives and newcomers in rural Provence, whether engaged in active farm production or a life of leisure. Nowhere is this more evident than in the properties—and gardens—of farmsteads and villages. Local landowners continue to mix fruit and flower in the old, unselfconscious manner; new residents find themselves drawn to, and deeply affected by, this rich heritage.

THE FARMSTEAD GARDEN

Frédéric Mistral, known by his colleagues as "The Poet of the Farm," helped create the idyllic image of Provençal country style. Remembering his childhood on "the Judge's farm" near Maillane, he wrote: "How cheerful, how whole-some was that scene of farm work; each season brought a new sequence of tasks. Plowing, sowing, shearing, mowing, the silkworms, the wheat harvest, the threshing, the wine harvest, the picking of olives—all displayed before my eyes the majesty of farm life, forever hard but forever independent and serene." When his father died, an inventory of household possessions was drawn up: pottery, furniture, fabrics, all useful, beautiful, handmade by expert craftsmen. Such objects can be seen again in their setting, reconstructions of old farmstead rooms, in the Arlatan museum in Arles that Mistral endowed; or the Demery factory in Tarascon, home of Souleiado textiles. Both places lovingly evoke farming's Golden Age in Provence.

The peak of prosperity was reached in the mid-nineteenth century, before the series of economic disasters that struck the region around 1870. Compounded by World War I and the rural exodus, these social changes marked the decline of a way of life that had existed for thousands of years. Today's farmsteads still benefit, however, from the millennia of agricultural experience that preceded them, even while undergoing radical change.

The first known agricultural community in France was founded in Courthézon, just northeast of Avignon, in 4650 B.C.

By the end of the Roman Empire, the best valley land belonged to huge estates, or *villae*. The most majestic of these were like palaces, and Pliny the Elder remarked that in them there was more to sweep than to plow. Their finery was financed by the crops they produced, however. Dependent on these domains in late Roman times were farmsteads called manses, consisting of a house, shelters for animals and harvests, a vegetable garden and an orchard. The common Provençal term *mas*, meaning farmstead, is said to derive from this. But although realtors today use the word all over the south, it traditionally refers only to the region of the Alpilles.

Today some farmsteads still have Roman foundations, especially along the Rhône, but most date from the sixteenth to the nineteenth centuries. The central unit of a traditional *mas*

The roof of a typical
Provençal mas *is made of rounded clay tiles of Roman inspiration,*
laid overlapping on a wooden frame.
Its angle is slight, as there is little snow in winter.

is a shoebox shape to which have been added, either in a line or around a central courtyard, many smaller cubes and rectangles. However large or small, farmsteads have always been situated with an eye to weather conditions, seasonal change, and the lay of the land. Here again practicality and pleasure are inseparable. The north wall has few windows, if any, to let in the mistral; in any case a tall hedge and perhaps the natural slope of the land protect it. The main façade faces south or southeast to catch the winter sun, but the famous trellis and large, carefully pruned deciduous trees (often planes or limes) provide dense summer shade.

This basic building lent itself to whatever transformations the fortunes of its owners might require. It generally would shelter a hayloft, a rabbit warren and a chicken coop, a barn for draft animals, cows and sheep, a cellar for making and storing wine, a pigeon coop that might be built into the roof and, nearby, a threshing floor and a well. Additions were made for new activities, the raising of silkworms for example, as of the eighteenth century. The larger farms also housed hired hands; and in the biggest domains were lodged artisans such as blacksmiths and carters, which explains the many outbuildings surrounding the larger estates.

Although the fields often came right up to the house terrace (as in the early Italian villas), many writers have left descriptions of ornamental planting, even on small properties. Willa Cather noted hollyhocks and sunflowers, Van Gogh admired roses, dahlias and pomegranates. Provençal novelist Henri Bosco succumbed to the seductions of a modest farm plot on the lower slopes of the Luberon: "The garden, nestled under the terrace, sheltered by high, warm walls but open onto the valley full of brown and blue summits, offered to the rosebushes, the tulips, and even to the stray weeds a well of warm air that smelled all at once of fruit trees, hawthorn and hyssop. Birds twittered among

*In this Alpilles farm garden
dating from the turn of the century, spring is long and full of flower: here can be
found rosemary, coronilla, Judas trees,
ornamental cherries, spring and summer tamarisks, paulownia, irises and roses.*

the plums. . . . Nothing was more charming than this garden. It existed in this tiny sheltered bit of land that had trusted itself to man, under the large benevolent house—just big enough for a soul without worldly ambition, or possessing the genius of retirement."

If many such souls now inhabit Provençal farmsteads, numerous local families still maintain elaborate gardens side by side with the commercial production of food crops. An estate in the Alpilles stands among its well-tended vineyards, with one of Provence's most famous hilltowns as a dramatic backdrop. This is a low building with a vast sloped roof sheltering the main residence, the working farm quarters and, for generations, an olive oil mill. The visitor approaching from the south veers left in front of the garden, past cypress sentinels, along a hedge of coronillas (fragrant gold in March and April) to the large courtyard where wine is sold. Much of the strictly private garden is visible as you pass.

The dominant feature here is a giant, well-pruned, canopied hackberry, with ivy twining up its massive trunk, flanked by boxwood carved into low banks and domes. The rest of the garden mixes somewhat random but charming shrub plantings including the most characteristic essences of the area: Judas trees, spring and summer blooming tamarisk, paulownia and a common jujube, irises and roses around an old

*Clipped greenery provides
an underlying structure and, beautifully set off by the coronilla hedge, frames this
Alpilles farmstead to perfection (top).
In its courtyard, an old stone trough brims over with annuals (above).*

millstone, more formal boxwood from which emerge the trunks of a pair of decorative cherry trees. The protected house terrace has a raised stone washing trough overflowing with primroses, an old well, urns that were once used for oil surrounded by rare crocuses in early spring, and a wall of climbing pale blue *Plumbago capensis* backing a Moroccan pool. Around the corner to the east are almond trees and rosemary near a larger well of rough-hewn stone. The broad eastern wall of the house, visible from the road beyond, was painted by Van Gogh.

A more modest but equally delightful example of a working farm is situated in the Gard, along a simple, flat valley road running between vineyards and cypress windbreaks. It belongs to a young couple in their twenties. The property once belonged to Mme. Rouméas's grandfather, and had not been lived in since the war. Her husband is a farmer, she works with a firm of landscape architects. They have just had their first child, whom she nursed while

relating the history of their garden. They kept, of course, the squared-off cypress hedge lining the road along the north side; but also the southern trellis, with its vines that give table grapes and a lovely rambling rose of unknown origin (similar to American Pillar, but not recurrent). A low wall separating terrace from field supports this structure, and under its shade there is now a series of tiny compartments paved with old tiles found in the house. The central space has been kept for a table and chairs made from the old beams of the house. Pots of all sizes mark transitions and passages.

Outside, the base of the low outer wall protects plumbago, lantana and tender sages. A fine *Salvia microphylla* contrasts with a pale violet delphinium. These grow all over the outer area, along with large clumps of single-blossomed hollyhocks in delicate colors. Beyond lie cultivated fields, and at their farthest boundary, the river.

The only access for tractor and trucks to the

In this young family's garden in the Gard,
beds of daisies planted under the low windows two generations earlier have been extended
with oleanders, germanders, day lilies, wild arums, plumbagos,
foxgloves, dianthus, and much more—all grown from seed or cuttings by the owners. Outside,
wild larkspur has been encouraged to spread (above).
The tamarisk, a tree that grows wild in the Camargue, remains a favorite of traditional
Provençal gardeners farther inland (opposite).

hen and baby chicks. Three horses feed in the meadow out front. There is even a rabbit, a pet, caged but kept, of course, in the garden.

Dozens of other farmsteads have been restored as vacation and retirement homes. Needs are different in this case, and after all, the wonderful local farmers' markets are only a village or a town away. The trellis may now shrink to reveal more of a beautiful façade, or it may be enriched with climbing English roses, passion flowers, *Campsis radicans* with its orange trumpets in summer or the more delicate pink version, *Podranea ricasoliana*. The southern terrace becomes a summer patio as much as a winter retreat. New French doors may allow more light inside, and create continuity between house and garden. In one case, Parisian owners have gone further still to make this connection: a suspended camera on the living-room ceiling projects television onto a large screen in the depths of the room, so that the owners of the *mas* and friends can watch while sitting

farm sheds is in the foreground. So that this driveway should not be a liability, it has been planted with a profusion of lavender, saponaria, oleander and coreopsis that give a riot of color in good farm garden tradition. A small collapsible swimming pool has been artfully disguised with flowering hibiscus and ricinus. This is a household full of vitality in which an old rosebush nudging the house terrace shelters a

*Two old roses commonly
found in the south: a single-flowered, once-blooming red climber and the
much-loved banksia (top and opposite).
Old farmsteads undergo many changes: vacation owners may add French doors
for easier garden access, but retain
the ancient shade trees that protect them from the summer sun (above).*

outside on the patio on warm summer evenings.

Outside, wells remain a prize feature; but where they have gone dry, they are covered with climbing roses or serve as planters. Large trees still shade at least part of the façade. The hedge or low wall that once separated the terrace from advancing fields often disappears, or becomes a pretext for elaborate plantings. Generally today people open up the spaces around the house and close off property limits, and if the house heats up, there is always the pool.

Luxury is not a new addition to life on the *mas*, however. The grandest have always been much like châteaux, stately homes for powerful landed gentry. Such is the case of a fourteenth-century property in the southern Alpilles with a famous Renaissance façade of cut stone, decorated with half columns. It was built for the wife of a governor of Les Baux and later housed a grand master of the Order of Malta, but no

title was ever attached to the land. The current owners created a garden of shrubs and perennials there some thirty years ago, keeping the veritable esplanade of plane trees in front of the *mas* (the trellis on a façade of these proportions can only be decorative). Astonishing, monumental yew topiary stand at each end of the rows of planes, their dense dark masses contrasting with the latter's variegated trunks and soaring branches.

The land here is unusually flat, and its divisions have been made clear by another formal feature of this garden: a series of sculpted, layered cypress hedges. These artfully placed dark green curtains provide special points of color, like the combined red and pink climbing roses that arch over the entrance to the vegetable garden. Their differences of height, the curves and angles of their shapes create movement, while their mass gives them a substantial presence.

The vegetable garden, a wonderful feature of this space, is almost completely enclosed by such hedging. Tomato stakes, artichokes, dahlias, lettuce, beans, roses for cutting, all lend themselves to geometries that are contained by lines of low, silver santolina that contrast with the tall cypresses, both squared and pointed. At the plot's southern limit, their dark foliage forms an arch, framing an urn and the cultivated fields beyond.

All the more detailed floral plantings benefit from this cypress backdrop, whether around the raised swimming pool with its millstone fountain, or in irregularly shaped beds nearer the house. Informal areas have been planted in the lawn that extends south of the plane-tree esplanade, visible through and under their canopies. Here isolated cypresses, oleanders, rosemaries, iris, peonies and varied perennials lead to the garden's southern limit, which is left open to the cultivated fields beyond. West of the house lie more winding flower beds planted around the workings of an old mill. This is the most protected part of the property, as is evident from the robust good health and size of a Japanese loquat (*Eriobotryra japonica*) underplanted with ivy. It shades the passage from terrace to garden. Beautifully pruned crape

Clipped cypress hedges in this southern
Alpilles garden limit visibility from one section to the next, never entirely hiding,
but always directing and framing views (above).
In front of a historic Renaissance façade, monumental yew topiary stand at each
end of a double row of planes for a striking effect (opposite).

myrtles with several trunks and tall spring-flowering brooms give height and volume to beds of iris, dianthus, peonies, arums, and roses.

This *mas*, like any château, has its working farm off to one side (with a lovely courtyard full of oleanders). Between it and the road, almond orchards make a spring garden, their delicate branches contrasting with the heavy limbs and leaves of an ancient spreading fig tree, which embraces an old stone well.

Much humbler beginnings can produce equally interesting results. West of the Rhône, in one of those delightful country villages that surround Uzès, a simple sheepfold dating from 1561 has become the focus for one of the richest contemporary southern gardens. Its models are both Turkish and Italian, though its planting was done with French help. The owner has sought to re-create some of the near-Eastern atmosphere of his origins, taking inspiration in particular from the sixteenth-century Turkish architect Sinan, who always planned the building and garden as a single entity. The heart of this property is a four-part courtyard surrounding a fountain. The house and its dependencies make up three sides of the quadrangle, with trellises on all three façades. These overflow with roses (Wedding Day battling with Virginia creeper), honeysuckles and jasmines. Through these the indoor spaces are extended into the garden, and indeed, thanks to their French doors, some rooms open as fully onto the garden as the latter's shaded spaces give onto its sunny center.

In the four formal sections, lavender and rosemary balls surround yew cones; the central fountain is an ivy ring with tall yellow and blue water irises clustering round the spout. A few steps on the open side of this quadrangle lead to another terrace slightly below; here olive trees are grouped in another four-part arrangement around large, Medici-style terracotta urns brimming with white geraniums. Two stone lions surrounded by foliage and flower mark the transition between these two main levels. Everywhere there are pots with subtle impatiens and fuchsias, daturas, pale geraniums, solanums and many rare plants from different parts of the world. These help create a layered effect in the garden, the highest point of which is a loggia with stone pillars on the west side. Pots with strongly structured plants like yuccas and tumbling geraniums climb their way toward this pinnacle, accentuated by a group of tall cypresses.

Two formal gateposts and a simple wrought-iron gate frame the furthest prospect south, which is open field. Cypresses serve both as a hedge and as focal points. Among them now grow tropical climbers raised from seed recuperated in Turkey, and nearby a group of yellow cassias, similarly obtained.

This garden is small but beautifully designed, and has other distinct and somewhat hidden spaces. On the right as you arrive, before reaching the main quadrangle, is a kind of wild garden in which phlomis and caryopteris thrive next to *Cuphea myrtifolia*, another cassia and a large red-leaved berberis. An unusual statue of a ram presides, framed in shrubbery from the house. Beyond the olive square is a white marble fountain from Istanbul (nineteenth-century Ottoman rococo) framed by a large violet lagerstroemia and evergreens. Hidden behind the fountain is a square space with a mosaic pebble paving in tones of gray and beige, a variation on the already salt-and-pepper—and cinnamon—tones of the building stones in this area. Its inspiration is the Topkapi palace in Istanbul. The entrance is graced by a Nevada rose, and beyond is a typical Mediterranean mixture of flower and fruit: medlar, pomegranates, quinces, *Abelia* "Edward Gaucher,"

In the old days, the wealth of a domain
was judged by the extent of its roofs. This property in the southern Alpilles
has kept an impressive expanse (above).
At the Bergerie du Bosquet, a former sheepfold near Uzès, stone steps
lead from the fountain level to another
terrace slightly below; here olive trees are grouped in another four-part
arrangement (opposite and following page).

variegated euonymus, cestrum and lemons in pots, pink hibiscus and cypresses, and rosemary. Below these creep pink verbenas, ivy, clumps of chrysanthemums, and much more.

This is a garden in which fragrance, touch and taste all have their place. There are no less than three outdoor dining spaces. One is shaded by the trellis closest to the main indoor area, another is on a raised terrace at the end of the house, also accessible directly from the living room. This is a particularly sheltered nook, protected by two large olives, cypress, eriobotrya, hippophäe and pittosporum, while on the house itself grows a rich wisteria and even a jacaranda. More pots, of course, including two finely sculpted urns. The third is a winter garden in the wing opposite, which can again be completely opened onto the outdoors in mild weather.

This property displays an unusual blend of influences, a discovery of possibilities in a site and structure that few people would have discerned. It is truly a paradise garden.

Farm buildings around an olive oil mill, a small family dwelling, a stately, sculpted stone residence, a vaulted sheepfold—these four examples lie on fairly flat land at the foot of nearby hills. Another converted farmstead lies on a steeper slope, not far from the approaches to the airy landscapes of Les Baux. The buildings are still extensive, horizontal and composed of many parts, but the garden's great sweep downward (in a flow, without terracing) is central to its design. The property thus nestles against the flank of a particularly wild *garrigue*

hillside, a dramatic backdrop for the manicured garden below. Its owner has combined here a great sensitivity to the Provençal setting with a passion for old roses.

The transition from the wilderness above to formality below, where trees, shrubs, and hedges are all beautifully pruned into smooth shapes, is striking. A slender, polished cypress stands against the abrupt *garrigue*, drawing the eye upward. Its line will be repeated by similar trees farther down the hill. Still at the garden's upper limit, however, where the hillside stops and lawn begins, stand other carefully shaped plants, horizontal in contrast to the cypress. A long, somber block of boxwood hedging makes a definite line, abruptly stopping before the cypress. And in front of this, two groupings stand like precious sculpture: pyracantha and Spanish broom (*Spartium junceum*). Neither are rare, of course—the latter could even be wild in this setting. Both flower at the same time, white and yellow. But the flattened, upside-down saucer shapes they have here assumed make them definitely part of the garden's more controlled domain.

Another subtle transition from wilderness to garden is achieved by the plantings around a stone shrine and statue of Saint James of Compostela. This friendly figure presides over a small rockery. One end of the rockery trails off toward the hilltop in a cloud of pale pink heuchera. Only a few yards farther on lies the south wall of the house, extended by an arbor covered with blue wisteria and yellow banksia roses, shaded by acacias, underplanted with agapanthus. Here too there is no abrupt separation between spaces, but a gentle passage from building to garden.

Similar care has been taken with the agricultural context—the olive orchards neighboring this property to the east. A cypress hedge separates the two domains, but it has been squared off low enough to allow the garden's olive trees, carefully rounded, to stand against those of the commercial plantation beyond, whose irregular domes are much the same size. This is typical of the kind of refinement found in this garden. Yet if each individual plant receives careful

*Two stone lions
guard the transition between the two levels of the Bergerie garden (above).
A poolside rock garden near Les Baux
displays a rich plant tapestry in muted colors against the wild
hillside in the background (opposite).*

guidance (a Mermaid rose is arched over wires in the middle of the lawn), all the lines of the garden's larger design are flowing rather than formal. They focus on two centers: above, the house with its adjacent swimming pool, and below, visible from all over, a sunken rectangle of rare old roses.

The house patio facing the pool is sheltered by an extended trellis covered with white wisteria. Fragrance wafts from a Zéphirine Drouhin rose and trachelospermum on the house walls, which also support New Dawn and a whole panel of *Plumbago capensis*. This is a delightful, private nook, an outdoor room for all times of year.

Descending from the house, one can see the lawn spreading out on both sides, slightly banked in places with mounds of lavender and helichrysum, with focal points such as the Mermaid and a flattened, oval-shaped raphiolepsis. In the distance, a group of pines with climbing

roses is outlined in a diamond point of gray santolina, sheltering the cutting garden. Beside this lies the rose rectangle, very much a collector's garden. Moss roses predominate on the path leading toward it, while it combines York and Lancaster (a favorite), Jacques Cartier, Yolande d'Aragon, Bella Doria and Rosa Mundi. In the sunken area, Centenaire de Lourdes has been planted at each end, Thérèse Bugnet all along the far side. There are some border roses like Milrose and Pink Ballerina, but also Cécile Brunner, Tricolor, Fantin-Latour. Even the cutting garden has Constance Spry, Souvenir de la Malmaison and a lovely golden climber of the Parure d'Or family.

This gardener prefers soft pastels, though she allows brighter yellows in the garden's wilder reaches. One of her prize combinations is a rare pale-flowered kolkwitzia with a Moonshine rose trailing through it, flowering simultaneously— white on white against a dark cypress hedge. Everything here is artfully planned; but the sense of control is not constraining since it is so carefully balanced with freer forms and lines, and since it is this garden's main inheritance from the agricultural tradition that lies, after all, just over the hedge and down the road. And although this is not a utilitarian garden in any sense, it is one in which fragrance has been given at least as large a place as appearance. The atmosphere is one of gracious well-being.

The Provençal farmstead has its basic conventions, its traditional orientation, construction, integration into its setting, but the variations on this theme effected by modern gardens are almost infinite. It is difficult to choose among so many examples, each with its own personality.

Decorator Jacques Grange has designed around a small, orange-tinted farmstead lying just under the crest of a hill near Saint-Rémy, a small garden whose several parts are a kind of resumé of traditional possibilities: there is the cypress lane underplanted with iris, leading to a gate that gives in turn onto a small field of lavender; a cherry orchard; an old fig tree encircling a well; a magnificent old hackberry and a well-pruned boxwood hedge, now

Decorator Jacques Grange's patio
makes the most of simple, traditional objects chosen with care and displayed
with pleasure. Bird cages and
their inhabitants add an unusual dimension (above and opposite).

sheltering the swimming pool. In the protected angle of the house, a comfortable patio under ancient shade trees sports not only pots of all sizes and stone troughs but decorative hanging bird cages.

This is a fairly modest property, though it contains a division of space by function worthy of great estates. Other farmsteads, while keeping their rustic character, are huge villages under one roof: the Mas Dalméran near Tarascon, for example, and the properties of the Crau or the Petite Camargue—both areas in which the old Roman villa estates have persisted. The Camargue, or delta area of the Rhône, possesses a character all its own, with its marshlands, rice paddies, wildlife, and "cowboy" culture. A famous raiser of bulls for the arena in Nîmes, Jean Lafont has transformed his ranch into a complex and detailed garden containing some thousand species and varieties of plants, but this is a property where one can get wet feet

even at the end of a drought-stricken summer. Bulls come to graze at the bottom of the garden. Fascinating as it is, this example belongs to another style of landscape.

The Petite Camargue contains the best of both worlds—the inland area and the delta. Here can be found a newly planted garden much more similar to those farther inland. It was designed by landscaper Emmanuel de Sauvebeuf. Built on the old vegetable plots and orchards of a nearby château (a property that has been in the owner's family for generations), it has been subdivided into three parts with modest differences of level. At the highest, west end was the old *noria*, a system for watering in which a mule turned round a well, raising and distributing the water in a sort of artisanal conveyor belt of goblets. Such constructions were common in this part of the Gard, and the nearby Château de Teillan has a particularly fine one. Today, however, these owners have incorporated its remnants into plantings around an ancient but recently purchased cutstone orangery, which looks as if it has always been on this spot. It is draped with banksia roses and enclosed in mixed shrubbery where cypress, *Melianthus major*, choisya and variegated ivy mingle shades of greens and whites and afford good wind protection.

All this provides backdrop for the massive stone fountain. In late summer this striking feature becomes even more imposing because of the pots of lotus it supports, which are going to seed in a truly spectacular manner. Clustered at the fountain's feet is a collection of old painted metal watering cans. Other plants provide similar strong lines: the melianthus, groupings of hostas, a wild shrubby polygonum with its shiny rods of black berries, and ricinus.

This fountain marks the transition to the second space, a large rectangle around a basin. The house closes one side of both these first sections, and along its considerable length runs a series of patios, winter gardens with a profusion of plants climbing pillars, tables and chairs, collections of frost-tender rarities and artfully displayed sculptures. The entire area has a sense of happy enclosure and protection, and its

The long farmhouse of Mr. C
in the Petite Camargue shelters a series of intimate corners,
each artfully arranged in a
blending of choice plants and decorative objects (above).
Mr. C's garden has several uncommon
architectural features, above all this elegant rotunda, backed by the old roof
tiles of the barn in which
the wine of the property is still made (opposite).

formal rectangular design, without ever becoming clouded, is softened by an impressive variety of plants—over a dozen different tree peonies, for example. Each season has its highlights, but this is a garden in which colors are plentiful, rich and warm.

The third and lowest area is the most dramatic: visible through a wrought-iron gate at the pool's end, a lane of cypresses leads to a round, colonnaded temple. Nothing too grandiose, but just the right proportions for the space. A mural fountain interrupts on the house side, set back to provide a short cross-axis. The hedge has been underplanted with lavender and yellow fall-blooming sternbergia. There are plans to alternate them with Anduze urns, set off by a geometric boxwood hedge. Windows in the latter will give views onto the garden on either side of the cypress lane, and these areas are already full of tree and shrub collections: lilacs of all descriptions, buddleias, rarities such as the pepper tree (*Schinus molle*), osage

orange (maclura), fragrant osmanthus and the too-seldom seen koelreuteria, with its delicate foliage colors in spring and fall and yellow summer bloom.

This garden excels at enhancing sculpted stone with a rich but controlled exuberance of vegetation. It might be thought that the landscaper, an antique dealer and decorator, was admirably placed to obtain the former, but it

*The heart of Mr. C's garden
is a formal rectangle surrounded by an exuberance of
delicate colors and shapes,
all receiving the same careful attention and placement
as the decor of the patios.*

seems that the latter falls into his domain as well: many of the plants in this garden have come from cuttings found on old properties of the region. The plant collections displayed in this garden are not therefore imitations of English models, but an extension of professional activity into private life—and perhaps also an echo of the southern tradition founded by experimentalists like Good King René and other château gardeners. But if decor and decoration are everything here (edible plants mostly excluded), the garden's main visual axis, the one lead-ing to the round temple, is stopped in the not too far distance by a mass of stone and old tiles: the barn where the wine of the property is still actively made and energetically marketed today.

These few samples give some idea of the range of valley farm gardens visible in the heart of Provence today. The same mix of rusticity and sophistication, often blended in surprising and original ways, characterizes the dramatic

mountain habitations, the hanging hilltowns that dominate the valley patchwork far below.

THE VILLAGE

Provençal villages are perhaps even more famous than valley farms for their picturesque harmony with the landscape. They evoke lyric descriptions even from geographers: in Henry Plummer's paean to southern French hilltowns in *Architecture* magazine (December 1986), he described them as "awesome sites, with deep emotional impact and concentrations of geological energy. . . ." He sees the human constructions as a kind of dynamic splitting of the earth's surface, creating "a variety of 'insides'. . . . where man can cling and dwell. . . . Fragmentary clusters of buildings interlace, pepper, and highlight the landscape, rather than coalesce into an absolute man-made island. Unlike more celebrated hilltop villages, like those in Italy with their tight crystalline masses and almost

The landscaper of this lovely garden, Emmanuel de Sauvebeuf, paid special attention to textural contrast, both foliage and mineral (above).

sculpted figures, these villages are openly arrayed and shuffled with the ground. Rock and vegetation permeate the town as a continuous presence. There results an exceptional rapport between settlement and earth."

Even in this elemental union with nature, history is a strong presence. The first southern hilltowns date, not surprisingly, from Neolithic times. Houses of stone were known in the south of France from the Bronze Age, and were grouped together by the time the Greeks came in 600 B.C. The Celts, arriving in the fourth and third century B.C., consolidated their *oppida* on the hilltops. Those of western Provence may have been elaborate trading communities, almost cities—the digs at Entremont near Aix bear witness to their activity. Other *oppida* existed near Orange, Carpentras, Cavaillon, Avignon, Arles. . . . Roman peace led to the organization of the lowlands, but during the decline of the Roman Empire, some mountain sites, like that of Bonnieux, were occupied once more. The town name of Oppède (in the Luberon) still evokes these ancient settlements.

The ambiguous term "villa" of the early Middle Ages seems to have applied to hilltowns as well as valley estates; by the tenth century, a new word, *castrum*, appears in the texts. Overlapping with "villa" for a time, it came to designate a private fortification, sometimes including a surrounding village. On the north slope of the Luberon, twelve castle sites still exist along a twenty-kilometer line running east-west. They bear witness to an expanding countryside that was dominated by a growing military aristocracy. Religious institutions provided a second pole of attraction for rural populations; where church and castle were united, villages were founded. This transformation of social structures was completed by the end of the twelfth century.

Subsequent history shows these sites were alternately deserted and revived. The Black Plague of the fourteenth century emptied many villages, but after the Hundred Years War, lay and church landowners alike encouraged repopulation, eager here as in the plains to re-use productive land. From this period too dates the

first "slippage" of villages down the slope. The final result was the low towns of the twentieth century that can be much more easily integrated into the communication networks of modern life.

As usual, there are highly practical reasons for these picturesque dispositions. Houses circle the site in descending rows, so that each level gets the maximum amount of sun and air; at the same time, narrow streets keep the village interior cool in the summer. This grouping of essentially vertical buildings is always asymmetrical; they may flow like the curving lid of an old-fashioned soup tureen, sit rigidly in a triangle, or dawdle like a flock of sheep scattered along a ridge. The curious, roughly triangular form of Mediterranean hilltowns inspired Cézanne in his search for geometric forms in nature, Picasso and Braque in their experiments with cubism. But one of their most interesting features is that they do change almost unrecognizably according to point of view. When approached from a road above on the flank of the hill or plateau, they may seem shapeless and lifeless, all their vitality directed toward the valley, whereas from below, they seem concentrated into a solid mass.

The essential unit of this collective construction is a narrow house, always linked to its neighbors by common walls. Many are built right onto the rock, and may even be cave dwellings with a masonry façade. This typical, vertical building sheltered just one family without servants or employees, and with only a few animals—a pig, perhaps, a mule, several sheep. The vaulted rooms of the ground floor sheltered these animals and the farm tools—but today house artisans and artists. Above was the narrow dwelling, with one or two unevenly spaced windows on the façade. At the very top was the attic, used for storage of wheat, raisins, figs, lentils, garlic and aromatic herbs.

The village ramparts, clearly visible from the valley, consisted of the outer ring of houses linked together. Circling these walls lay small vegetable plots for immediate supply, with the main crops grown farther down the slopes. Pagnol describes how, around a typical village,

*Provençal hilltowns like Bonnieux
are among the landscape's most picturesque features. Many today are full of
colorful pocket plantings and greenery
that cascades over the old walls of secret gardens.*

"thanks to connections made to the pipeline to the fountain, there were rich vegetable gardens greening, and orchards of peaches and apricots, whose fruits were taken to the market." Most villagers were independent landowners at least of these small plots, but the collectivity was a strong binding force.

Today, village streets are filled with a great variety of pocket gardens: old stone mangers overflowing with verbena and geraniums, vines and roses climbing walls, often growing out of tiny cracks in the pavement or between cobblestones. Certainly all village gardens involve differences of level and strong mineral elements. They cannot but be architectural. Views are also inevitable, except in the most enclosed courtyards. In most cases, owners buy two or more adjoining houses with common walls, and open these into one extended dwelling. Parts of the original constructions that are in ruins become protected garden spaces, an original sort of garden "room," the simplest and most effective way of moving from indoors to patio and garden.

One such property has been restored by Monsieur and Madame Barjou in a village east of Avignon that has fine mountain views in all directions. Nestled under the town ramparts, this garden has been made over quite a large area on the north slope. The rose-covered gate that opens onto the street gives no indication of the volumes within. The house itself has been largely rebuilt, and walls from the unrestored ruins adjacent have been retained to make a three-sided winter garden. A climbing crimson

rose draws the eye to a ruined tower in the far corner, behind the mulberry and almond trees that shelter a table for summer dining.

One leaves this enclosed patio through a stone arch to the north: beyond, one discovers a terraced hillside with many connections, layers, low and high walls, passages, open and sheltered spaces, and a number of different, never symmetrical levels. All the plantings are simple and local, including those in pots here and there, on a wall or at a junction. Structure is given by the stone, but also by good use of corresponding and contrasting dark foliage shapes, cypress towers and low boxwood planters in strategic places.

A long set of curving stone steps descends to a kind of secret garden, past a cluster of white lilacs. From the bottom one can look back and see all levels telescoped, with cistus, rosemary, sage, lavender, centranthus overflowing from one wall to the next and iris bands lining the walls. *Celtis australis*, the beloved hackberry, casts welcome shade in some spots. But if instead of descending one continues on the top level, one arrives at another patio area under a trellis, with table and chairs, and views both on the vertical garden below and across the valley toward the mountains beyond. Nothing feels cramped—there is a comfortable balance of open vistas and shelter, and also a delightful sense of discovery. The stonework itself definitely provides the garden's main theme, with its steps, walls, gateways. Plantings are valued as much for their foliage as their flowers (grays and greens often juxtaposed); floral colors are generally discreet, taken from the natural, spontaneous vegetation.

This property shows how Provençal village fragments can be transformed into a garden: ruins, instead of being abandoned or rebuilt, can be turned into a sculptural itinerary of patterns, stone and vegetation constantly embracing.

Madame Barjou considers hers a "poor" garden, made without the resources available to the international magnates, movie producers, stars, media personalities, politicians, financiers, successful writers and artists who people

Madame B has created a lovely,
simple arrangement of cineraria and green santolinas around earthenware jars
containing nothing but sculpted box (above).
The steep slope of Madame B's garden offers stunning views in addition to
sheltered nooks on various levels (opposite).

these towns. It is certainly true that the most fashionable perched villages of inland Provence lie all around her, on either side of the Calavon river, whose broad valley east of Avignon provides some of the finest Provençal farmland patchwork. To the north, on the Vaucluse plateau, Gordes is among the most sought-after communities, perhaps because of its original celebrity as an artist's town: cubist painter André Lhôte discovered it just before the war, and Vasarely opened a museum in the town's Renaissance château in 1970. To the south lies the dark, dramatic range of the Luberon. Its steep northern slopes have their own lofty villages that are, if anything, even more prized by cosmopolitan celebrities. Their settings are particularly abrupt and remote, having often served as fortresses during the bitter sixteenth-century wars of religion, when they were besieged by the bloodthirsty baron of Oppède. This latter village was destined to become yet another artists' and writers' colony during

the last war, when Consuelo de Saint-Exupéry devoted herself to creating a new community of troubadours there. Then there is nearby Lacoste, with its ruined castle of the Marquis de Sade, its summer art institute and its dramatic abandoned quarries; Bonnieux, with its neighboring prehistoric digs and nineteenth-century forest of Atlas cedars; Ménerbes, whose profile evokes a ship wrecked on the summit—these must count among the most famous of Provençal hill-towns. Nicolas de Staël settled in Ménerbes, whose citadel was restored by Impressionist art historian John Rewald. Its garden has retained a succession of fortified terraces: the highest and smallest lies at the foot of a Carolingian watchtower; the broadest and lowest, near the massive dwelling, surrounds a small turquoise pool sheltered by cypresses with raised flower beds.

One of the more ambitious gardens of this area complements an entire hamlet restored by Dominique Cornwell. This fortified enclave and

*The medieval fortress citadel
of Ménerbes contains within its narrow walled garden all modern
comforts, even a swimming pool.
Spectacular seen from the valley, from its ramparts this castle
provides magnificent views
of the farmland below (above and opposite, top).*

its land cover about eighteen acres. Here the garden design includes orchards and vineyards, since the house (now composed of several units, restored and connected) looks both down on the valley below and toward the village of Gordes perched above. The site is world famous, and protected by the Caisse Nationale des Monuments Historiques. Two landscape architects have worked on this garden (J. P. Carayon and

Philippe Cadoret) under the owner's direction. It was decided to strengthen the existing plan rather than try to impose a new one.

The first landscaper designed the pool as an extension of the main living room, creating a ground-cover composition on the surrounding terraces. Low sculpted box in geometric patterns reinforces the lines of the pool, seconded by evergreen mounds of santolinas, cotoneasters, junipers along the paths and roads, and highlighted by cascades of white flowers (geraniums, impatiens) in large pots. Some majestic, white-flowering horse chestnuts were retained. The second specialist proposed extending the pool axis westward up an incline, between regularly spaced cypresses and olives, to frame an arbor covered with white roses—all of this to be profiled against Gordes rising beyond, topped by its wrought-iron church belfry. The owner, wisely perhaps, felt this composition too monumental for a country village setting, and chose as a focal point, instead of the arbor, a particu-

*Dominique Cornwell has transformed
a hamlet near Gordes into an original residence and extensive garden
combining formal design and country traditions (above).*

larly fine, big eight-hundred-year-old olive tree.

The decisions made in the planning of this property took into consideration the model of château gardens on the one hand, and the site's original agricultural vocation on the other. Happily both can be suggested and incorporated in the final design, particularly in the new parterre below the pool, a foreground for the orchards and vineyards that extend for quite a distance beyond the hamlet itself. Situated here, visible from the formal swimming pool terrace, a four-part arrangement of santolinas has been planted, echoing both the box labyrinths familiar in the bastide gardens of Aix and the patterns of the neighboring fields. White gravel fills in the spaces, edged with rounded olive trees on their outer limits with low boxwood balls along the paths. A medieval stone well stands at the center of this composition.

Inspiration for this garden has remained resolutely Mediterranean, in spite of the owner's English connections. Its formal designs

can be seen from all over the valley and must have strong lines. This is a garden of greens, silvers and whites, with golden stone providing warmth and luminosity. This entire garden (except for some of the inner courtyards of the house complex itself) must count as one of the most visible, public and spectacular of Provence.

Some degree of open-endedness, as has already been observed, characterizes the typical Provençal garden. Rare indeed are those properties even today that do not include the outside world, even if only as a sea of tiled roofs adjoining a city courtyard. One interesting exception has been created by Michel Semini, Parisian landscape designer, for his summer home in Goult. Here for once the view—available everywhere from the town—is excluded from the garden, which takes advantage rather of the encircling and enclosing nature of village topography. Nothing from the street outside leads you to expect the artful plantings hidden

The Cornwell garden's main axis is an avenue
of cypress and olive trees leading up the hill toward the village (above).
A beautifully sculpted Anduze pot
links olives and cypresses in this garden, in which all bloom
provides pale accent for foliage (opposite).

behind the high wall in the large inner courtyard.

This is a highly controlled garden with an unusual richness of foliage texture and bloom. Banks of strongly pruned *Ceanothus thyrsiflorus repens*, mock orange and osmanthus provide layers of seasonal fragrance and color as you mount a small, steep path to the main level. Here the swimming pool has been turned into a central feature—again, contrary to usual practice. The modern stone slabs that surround it blend imperceptibly with old ones of the same color closer to the house (the original house terrace); grass is allowed to grow in the cracks behind these, which are also slightly higher than the pool. Once the entrance steps have been mounted, this is the only difference of level in this atypical garden.

A low thuya hedge punctuated by two pencil cypresses at each end masks the transition from pool to house in the middle, while the main path leading inward is sheltered by the spreading branches of a large Chinese mulberry. The building seems partly to enclose the pool, but its indoor spaces, thanks to shading plants and roof overhangs, are not clearly separate from the outdoor room. Indeed, at the far end, a large barn has been left without its façade, so that it is entirely open to the garden; its roof has been redone with old tiles but also with glass panes to let in filtered light. Its walls are lined with low-slung couches, and indirect lighting (hidden in large Anduze pots like those outside) illuminates a raised cactus garden. The sculptural effects of this are enhanced by the roots of an old ivy plant embedded in the stone wall behind.

Outdoors, greens dominate both furnishings and plantings but are lit by spots of color at different times of year: blue and white in spring, red in summer. Geraniums and oleanders are used with discretion.

This garden is completely surrounded by high walls, and in the space between them and the central pool, some rural elements have been retained as focal points: an old cistern stands with its pump to one side, under an arch backed now with bamboo and pittosporum. The right angle connecting barn and house is sof-

tened by a fountain, its low wall edged with red and white potted geraniums, its water spouting from two grotesque faces on the wall above. Each space is intimate and public at the same time; each has its own emphasis, but its boundaries are fluid. Even the low planes of the house roof maintain the sense of ambiguous flow: it is not immediately clear that they double as upper patios, but this uncertainty is intriguing rather than unsettling. In this garden, traditional village features have been absorbed to enhance the enjoyment of a self-contained world.

In contrast, consider the opposite effects obtained in another highly original example, also lying in the heart of a medieval village, encircled by its ramparts as they descend from the summit. It exists on no less than six levels! Everything predisposes it to verticality, and indeed the high walls provide a solid stone backdrop much as in an ancient theater. But this garden's most striking feature is resolutely horizontal. It lies below the house terrace, down a short, broad, formal flight of steps guarded by a pair of English stone lions (their Florentine counterparts preside farther along). This is an acacia walk, a long and impressive avenue with pots of red geraniums for punctuation, which has such perfect scale that the whole thing seems much larger than it really is. Two ties with the garden's agricultural past have been included in this almost French formality: one almond and one cherry tree are now surrounded by low box hedging.

On the avenue's outer edge (never very far away, in fact) is a varied view of the valley and the roofs below. On the inner side, the high back wall shelters cypress columns, stone benches and above all, elaborate drystone patterning, sometimes in the old herring-bone design. The stonework here is less rustic than in many other gardens, and more golden. The owners love sculpture, and have chosen a site that is itself a piece of natural sculpture, a remarkable blend of privacy and openness.

Not all village gardens are crowded inside the narrow confines of medieval ramparts. Some on the contrary have been created on the

A formal acacia walk in the heart of a Vaucluse village garden lies below the house terrace, guarded by a pair of English stone lions.

edges of towns, where there is considerable freedom from constricting neighbors. Many of these communities contain numerous outlying hamlets, some quite isolated, all secretive and full of elaborate private gardens. One such example has been restored as an extended family dwelling surrounded by a "wild garden," southern style. For example, a natural wood of green oaks near the entrance has been pruned to show off the rhythms of their trunks, underplanted with a low-clipped boxwood hedge. The garden here is a concentration of the wild *garrigue* into the sheltering oasis of the hamlet's drystone walls. The main feature is a round basin, edged with the rough slate of the countryside. The Luberon slumbers heavily on the horizon, while all around are artfully placed rock piles and *garrigue* plants that echo the larger shapes and natural vegetation of the outer landscape. Everything here is subtle beige, pale green, gray and gold; stone, foliage and water blending. The latter stands out from the rest by

its different motion when the wind is blowing. Otherwise, its reflections integrate it even further into the setting.

These few examples all belong to the picturesque hilltowns of the Vaucluse range and the Luberon that not only contain some of the most sophisticated personal creations, but often seem like large public gardens in their own right. In Roussillon, where waves of passing tourists and residential artisans have not entirely destroyed village simplicity, almost any greenery looks good against the ocher and orange tints that have made this village so famous. Small restaurants have made the most of its ancient trellising, and planter boxes splurge with floral color, here as elsewhere, wherever a few centimeters of earth will allow. In such communities, individual owners combine efforts to encourage ornamental plantings. Departmental and national prizes are offered for the best efforts. These floral pots and pockets bring out the surprising asymmetries and differences of levels in village

*This isolated garden
is a concentration of the wild* garrigue *into the sheltering oasis
of the hamlet's drystone walls.*

110

building, where all street gardens are tiny and cascading.

If these valley towns currently draw the most cosmopolitan settlers, other areas in the heart of Provence contain hilltowns just as beautiful and virtually unknown to outsiders. Auron, a village between the Durance river and Aix, is a typical example. The site was occupied in prehistoric and Roman times, but took its current form in the eleventh century. Like so many others in the area, it has prehistoric grottoes, vestiges of a Roman villa, a ruined castle built partway into the rock. . . . Parts of a seventeenth-century château also remain, particularly a long row of Ionic columns on top of a low retaining wall, curving down a village street and framing a series of small gardens below. There is a modest Romanesque church with an arched belltower.

On the southern edge of Auron, where the pine forest gives way to stone terracing, stands an old, huge plane tree so tempting and easy to

climb that people take pictures of each other sitting in its heart. In its shade lies the old washing-trough, and behind this a small, bright, public garden. There are large trees everywhere in the town: mulberry, hackberry and plane, shading the several streets that meander up to the summit. Courtyards are often visible from above, some old, some in the modern villa style, all full of flowers, some colorful as well from hanging laundry. The townspeople have everywhere planted cascading vines and roses, hollyhocks in mere handfuls of earth. But there is more variety here than in the average village: the hollyhocks are seconded by snapdragons; scooped-out walls turned into planters contain not only geraniums but also sedums, zinnias, miniature roses, portulaca. A shaded crack between wall and road protects a deep red dahlia on a bed of pale yellow and purple violets. A grouping of copper green urns on steps contains *Sedum spectabile*, its changing tints echoing the subtleties of the pots. Between two shallow

The round pool reflects its wild setting; in this garden, stone dominates a vegetation that manifests more beige and gray than green.

Clematis montana rubens and guarded by a sculpted choisya. An assemblage of earthenware pots contains a collection of scented pelargoniums. In various spots the pink flowers of *Polystichum latifolium* contrast with its silver foliage, blooming generously all summer. A narrow space on a high wall next to the mounting steps has a Crimson Glory rose above the violet potato blossoms of a *Solanum rantonnettii*, pruned into a pillar shape but flowering profusely nonetheless. At the top of these steps, a *Podranea ricasoliana*, with its delicate leaves and pink trumpets, covers a corner above pink hibiscus and oleander. Colors here are once again subtle whites and pastels, even grays, which suit the filtered light. The rich blend of plants also gives off a wealth of perfumes. . . .

The upper terrace is still being planted, its three walls providing protection for many rarities. A large window framing a plunging view of the valley below has been glassed in. This garden too has achieved that magic balance between openness onto a vast world outside and enclosure, shelter and intimacy that marks the best of the village gardens.

Although Villeneuve-les-Avignon (across the river from the papal city) is already something of a town, some of its gardens are very similar to their village cousins, tumbling down steep cliffs, making the most of tiny terraced spaces with superb views. A visitor walking up toward the Fortress of Saint-André goes through a street of elegant stone houses with high walls and gates, passing many typical village pocket plantings along the way. Some fine gardens lie

stone buttresses, a *Cotoneaster horizontalis* fans out behind more sedum, leaning on a young cypress and accentuated by a single pale pink geranium. All this can be found in the midst of a drought-stricken summer.

Still in this northern section of Provence but farther west, dominating the Rhône valley near Bollène and the nuclear plant of Pierrelatte, La Garde Adhémar hides within its folds numerous pockets of color and greenery. An elegant garden of rare plants has been designed here by Anne Simonet, a writer and journalist specializing in gardens. Constructed once again on the several levels of a neighboring house fallen into ruins, it covers a small area, essentially a courtyard. Low pieces of wall have been left in strategic places to become dividers and even, when topped with stone mangers, planter boxes for bulbs and sedums. A large gate (deliberately painted in the turquoise tones of faded copper sulfate spray) separates this private world from the street while letting it be glimpsed just enough that passersby are always asking permission to look. A majestic, fragrant linden tree provides a shady transition between street and entrance, wind protection and a kind of encircling security for the levels that rise opposite it.

The walls of this garden have been used for maximum effect: winter jasmine intertwines with *Jasminum mesnyi* across from the entrance, *Clematis alpina* and roses climb on deep blue trellising. Shaded corners are lightened by white bleeding heart, fuchsias, and a collection of hostas, variegated myrtles and the climbing rose Clair Matin. The house door is framed by a

From the top level of Mr. Kiener's terraced garden, a shaded patio covered with climbing polygonum faces the steep valley beyond (top). In the same village, Bernard Devaux has created winding paths through an olive orchard dotted with islands of irises among cistus, sage, achilleas, santolinas, hypericums, oleanders, and rosemary (above).

behind these walls, untouched by modern fashions. Those that circle upward to the left are connected by a series of small gates, lanes and trellises giving at the end of the line onto a vast olive orchard just below the turrets of the fortress. Those that occupy the downward slope to the right are so hooked into the hillside that parts of the houses are troglodyte dwellings and old quarries. The best of these reproduces in miniature some features of the great abbey garden on the hill above: a formal parterre with roses edged in santolina, cypress hedges, and a view onto the Pope's Palace across the river. But it also has the gentle clutter of fruit trees, rosemary, iris, lavender, perennials and pergolas that belongs to the Provençal country garden. From its lower levels one can see the neighbors' steep retaining walls with their flowering terraces.

Today, even the most sophisticated farm and village gardens still have their roots in the soil. These ancient sites remain rural, however much inhabited by jet-set personalities. The churches with their wrought-iron bird-cage belfries are still in use, for the most part. Nevertheless, there have been many changes since twelfth-century peasants clustered around the village church and castle to form communities. The castles have undergone important transformations— some ruined, some reconverted. The world of Provençal châteaux today ranges from these ancient battlements to elegant neoclassical residences and vast agricultural domains. These generally house a more old-fashioned elite than

the newly restored *mas* and fashionable villages: many are still occupied by the same old families for whom they were built centuries ago. But here too, within certain common patterns, there is an imposing variety both in the vestiges of past ages and in the solutions people have found for gardening on these sites.

*In Roussillon, the red roses surrounding
the town hall's front door have been photographed countless times,
but still delight many a passerby.*

CASTLES IN PROVENCE

The castles of Provence are among the region's most secret treasures: generally private, often small-scaled enough to disappear behind a grove of stately trees at the juncture of fields and pastures. And yet their relation to the land has been primordial. Provençal nobility vied throughout the centuries among themselves, with the church, and with city administrations for power over the earth's production. At the same time, they participated in the larger political struggles that constantly opposed northern and southern Europe and often centered on Provence. Thus situated between France and Italy, they could look in both directions for new models in both architecture and gardens. Here as elsewhere, château owners created the most cosmopolitan of ornamental decors—a role assumed more and more today by the internationally based elite that is restoring farmsteads and village homes. Even when outside influences were strongest, however, Provençal landed gentry have always had a reputation for remaining close to the land and tuned to its seasons.

Elegance and earthiness—château life, Provençal-style, has held great romantic appeal for writers. Lawrence Durrell, drawing no doubt on several models, imagined a typical example in the Verfeuille of his *Avignon Quintet*. Its twelfth-century keep stands above "a comfortable dwelling merging into a farmhouse with all its clumsy dependencies—barns and stables, wine-magazines and olive presses." Extensive formal gardens "decline southward and westward and are well sheltered from the sudden inclemencies of the Provençal weather, abounding in balustraded terraces and ornate stone benches perched at strategic points. Here and there you could happen upon a marble nymph or two in a debased and old-fashioned style, though now made really charming because overgrown by ivy or rambler roses. Here were many sheltered corners which one watched covetously for the first violets or the tender spring flowers; while along their length the beehives stood in rows. . . ."

The admiring author adds that "once all this was a profitable and lovely demesne," lost now

because of children who have studied in London and Paris and regard Verfeuille as a vacation home rather than a working estate. He judges it "more beautiful because of the neglect, though no farmer would have said so. . . ."

He was certainly correct in that conclusion, but luckily not all of these properties have fallen into disrepair. And the close connections between gentry and peasantry that Frédéric Mistral described so proudly still persist in many respects. It is perhaps this propinquity that causes many people to remark, even today, that Provence is a "poor" country, with no time or wealth for such frivolities as gardens. But a moment's glance at the region's history reveals a number of powerful dynasties that exploited land through the centuries, building lordly residences according to the customs of the times, often owning a good number at once. Some of these families were patrons of troubadours (or even troubadours themselves), holding courts famous all over Europe. But even in that glorious, far-off, late medieval period, northern knights scorned southerners for behaving too much like peasants, not enough like lords. In 1235, Raimond Bérenger V, Count of Provence, passed a decree forbidding his knights, and their sons and nephews, "to plow, to dig the earth and to transport by donkey either wood or manure." Were these activities proof of poverty, evidence of a shameful lack of standards? Or simply the persistence of another tradition? Fernand Benoit, the southern historian who records this instance, concludes proudly that in Provence, "the noble and the peasant speak the same language, have the same mores and the same preoccupations."

Once again there is a problem of definition. Provençal château gardens, like the Italian villas that are in many ways their counterparts, mixed ornament and agriculture in accordance with ancient Mediterranean custom, not because they could not afford better. Northern nobility came to regard a separation of the useful from the decorative as proof of prestige: as of the Renaissance, they banished the grapevine from their gardens as a plant too humble for aristocratic pretensions. These domains, especially

*Medieval battlements
create impressive silhouettes on hilltops all over Provence, but are hard to
maintain in modern times.
The castle of Le Barroux has become an international study center.*

the regal properties of the Loire valley, became the model and the standard all over Europe. Indeed, for French monarchs, refinement lay in making such distinctions in all domains of art and culture: thus they opposed tragedy and comedy (avoiding the abominations of a Shakespeare), and sweet ingredients from savory in their cuisine. (Provençal cooking still puts raisins and almonds into spinach pies.)

In the south, the model remained predominantly Roman. Sidonie Apollinarus described with admiration a fifth-century property of the Languedoc, one of the huge estates that controlled the best valley land at the end of the empire: "What a superb aspect it offers the eyes! Its temple, its porticoes, its magnificent baths make it shine from afar and the fields, the waters, the vineyards, the olive orchards, the vestibule, the plain, the hillside add to its pleasures." Southern domains kept their grapevines and fruit trees even near extravagant *folies* of the most French inspiration.

The feudal system never took hold as completely in the south as in the north. Since according to Roman law all the children of a noble family shared the inheritance (even women, unless they received a dowry at marriage), it was rare for southerners to build estates as vast as those of the north—one reason, perhaps, why landowners remained much closer to the actual work of the land. In later centuries, southern lords gained prestige for their agricultural experimentation and curiosity about new plants, both useful and decorative. This was true of the fifteenth-century Count of Provence, Good King René, whose career was marked by a great capacity for the good life, all manner of festivities, refinement in the arts—and military defeat. A lover of pageantry that was archaic even for his time, René spent many of his later years in his ten royal residences in Provence. At Gardanne he enlarged a simple bastide that became the center of a working experimental farm. There were oxen for plowing, milk cows,

Garden sculpture remained popular near Aix, even though out of fashion in the north, and was more directly inspired by antiquity. These delightful lovers are at La Mignarde.

many goats and some thirteen hundred sheep—attended by shepherds and shepherdesses in elegant, beribboned livery. There was a menagerie containing not only the usual lions and tigers but gazelles, camels, and an elephant. The royal residence was kept full of flowers and sweet-smelling herbs, which delighted the many young ladies that René invited to inspect it.

King René, it is sometimes said, was not really a southerner—after all, he preferred Anjou wines and walnut oil to the local products! But his activities in Provence were in keeping with the southern tradition of lords taking real interest in land management, one that today's landed gentry still practices with easy familiarity.

In the centuries that followed, wealthy Provençal landowners gained titles by having their country properties "enfeoffed," their owners paying homage and often tribute to a powerful noble or bishop who in turn conferred a title that would be attached to the land. A necessary condition of such a bargain was, almost invariably, the construction of a lordly residence. This system was in place everywhere, of course; but perhaps because Provence slumbered so far from the northern centers of power, or because individual estates usually remained small and today are still discreetly and privately held, their great number and variety is not generally acknowledged. They range from the fortified pile of stones which, even when still inhabited, can barely be distinguished from the rock on which it stands, to elegant neoclassical, French-inspired domains and manor houses that are like large, imposing farmsteads. Many, of course, incorporate styles from successive centuries and other places. But they either dominate, or nestle among the cultivated fields that have always been their *raison d'être*.

BY HIGH CASTLE WALLS

The first *castra* were simply fortified sites, which probably did not include a garden courtyard until the late Middle Ages. Their ruins commonly deck hilltops all over Provence today, sometimes looking like pieces of natural outcroppings, still impressive seen from valley roads even if these have now become freeways.

Many waves of destruction produced these picturesque effects: the Albigensian Crusade; marauding mercenaries in the fourteenth century and the desolation that followed the Black Plague; fanatical attacks in the sixteenth century between Catholics and Protestants, which often lay waste to whole communities as well as the castle they surrounded; systematic destruction by the ministers of Louis XIII and Louis XIV of major provincial strongholds; the Revolution, which left such strange architectural vestiges at the Tour d'Aigues, but nothing of its elaborate garden; and, not least, the German army of occupation. Today, stony spikes stand against the sky like broken teeth at Lacoste, Châteauneuf-du-Pape, Vaison-la-Romaine, and at the Fontaine-de-Vaucluse, the latter a castle where Petrarch went to dine.

And yet so much remains—still, in some

The celebrated Good King René had many castles and domains. One former hunting lodge, the Château de Breuil in the Alpilles, today features elegant sculpture and two imposing avenues of plane trees.

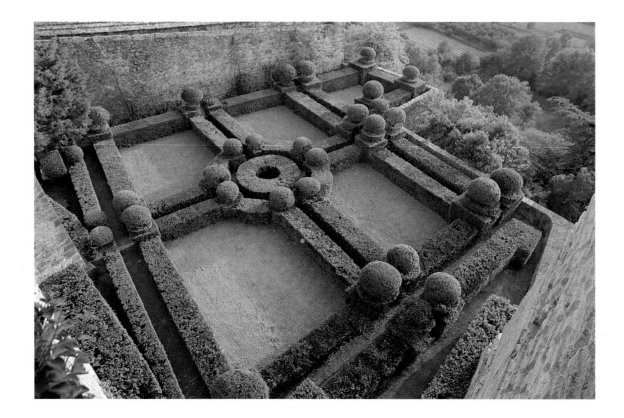

cases, belonging to families that have occupied the same site since the twelfth century. Some of these are struggling today to restore and maintain their châteaux and land—with gardens. The medieval keeps are perhaps the most difficult of all to preserve, and those that survive have met with different destinies: at Le Barroux, an international center for foreign students has been established; at Suze-la-Rousse, an ultramodern wine university is planting experimental gardens with many different varieties of grapes on the slopes below the castle. Several keeps acquired new battlements, or at least crenellations, in the nineteenth century, when their medieval charms became Romantic decors.

Probably the most famous example still surviving is the magnificent castle of Ansouis. Built like many others on the site of a Celtic *oppidum*, it must also have been a Greek stronghold—indicated by the discovery there of a treasure of silver drachmas. Once the home of

two saints and four queens, this castle was constructed between the tenth and sixteenth centuries from the same golden stone that embellishes many elegant residences in and around Aix-en-Provence. Its forms evolved so much in each succeeding period that today, as one architect said, its internal connections are like Swiss cheese. Perched on a rock from which the Alps are sometimes visible, it offers small room for gardens. And yet that little space has been used for maximum profit. The narrow terraces with their dramatic stone buttressing were filled in from the sixteenth to the eighteenth centuries, and outer battlements were replaced with boxwood parterres. Its pentagonal basin is linked by a canal to a Roman reservoir. To the east lies the Peiresc garden, named for the botanist who, like Olivier de Serres in the same period, was a great experimental gardener. This series of narrow terraces is best viewed from the ramp above. Its boxwood has retained its curious, not quite symmetrical shape, and

*The Paradise garden at Ansouis,
named for the cemetery it replaced, was designed for a narrow terrace
at the foot of the battlements.*

indeed has grown too large for the space provided. To the west, near the church below, is the Paradise garden, so named because its plot was once a cemetery. The box here has more sober lines, with circles in the center, rounded corners, and small domes, reminiscent of northern styles. This design is also meant to be seen from the balcony. The main entrance, facing south, has the broad, shaded, terraced courtyard characteristic of most Provençal domains, extended and enhanced here by massive, three-tiered box towers.

In the valley far below lies another part of the gardens, linked to the castle by the dramatic ramp described earlier. In this strictly private territory, a large, rectangular Roman basin became a Renaissance foreground for a high wall with a nymphaea and attendant statuary. Now it has evolved into a modern swimming pool, bordered with colorful lagerstroemia and beautiful day lilies. Recently planted groupings of birch and cypress give height to the composition.

The Sabran-Ponteves family that enjoys these gardens has devoted tremendous resources to their restoration. Though the property at one point passed into other hands, the current owners are the descendants of those for whom the castle was built. The late duchess and her husband devoted their lives to its preservation after three generations of neglect. The work involved was tremendous. Nineteenth-century taste had seen fit to plant four northern pines in the midst of the boxwood *broderies* of the Paradise garden. The Duke once proposed to his wife, as an extravagant Christmas present, the removal of these trees. She accepted with alacrity.

Watchtower castles can be particularly exposed to wind, of course, though they often have fine protected spaces as well. The castle of

Edged in box, the pentagonal basin at Ansouis is clearly visible from the ramparts of the château high above.

Issarts can be so battered by the mistral that a former chatelaine claimed she could not go into the chapel in the park without being blown right up to the altar. Today this is a garden with several levels and many facets. The Forbin family that still inhabits this property (another of the great noble dynasties of Provence) has tried to soften the austerity of the ancient keep by planting summer flowers along its walls: even plumbagos and lantanas thrive here, with bedding plants. Oleanders add more color, along with the traditional geraniums in Anduze pots. A simple square where the driveway meets the esplanade in front of the château is planted with *Ceratostigma plumbago* and edged with santolina—a very effective combination.

The southern hillside is terraced: simple parterres lie below the esplanade with four immense nineteenth-century cedars among them (two deodara Himalayas, two Atlas); farther down is a typical park planting of high

evergreen shrubs laced with walkways. Finally, lowest of all, are wild *garrigue* areas that the daughters of the family are now transforming into modern shrubberies with benches. Here a viewpoint is surrounded with iris, oleanders, olives, ruscus, *Arbutus unedo*, and koelreuteria, mixed with wild vegetation. The steep northern slope behind the château has also been improved: its natural boxwood clusters are now interplanted with occasional oleanders, iris, euphorbias, and yuccas. It has become the civilized counterpart of the *garrigue* just across the narrow valley, with its stony outcroppings, box, bupleurum and parasol pines. Unfortunately, the new fast train line threatens to completely transform this wild landscape, passing at the very foot of the château.

Many other examples of restored battlements persist today: Donzère in the heart of its village, with its wooded hillside full of ruins, splendid cedars, and rare irises; Uzès, where the descendant of an ancient lineage has installed a wax museum to evoke his Duchy's history, and organizes theatrical and musical spectacles and formal receptions in the gardens; Vaison-la-Romaine, a private enclosure of steep, hidden spaces giving onto vast vistas, where Roman and medieval fragments emerge among the oaks and cypresses of an abandoned park.

Fontarèches, transformed in modern times with English climbing roses and flower beds, has maintained an impressive labyrinth under tall oaks. A Marseille landscaper, Robert Bigonet, has designed a delightful blending of Mediterranean shrubs and perennials around an ele-

*The centuries-old topiary
at Ansouis has reached massive proportions (top).
The Château de Fontarèches
still has its impressive labyrinth under tall oaks (above).*

gant, half-sunken stone pool house designed by Hervé Pouzet des Iles. But originally, the property of Fontarèches, like that at the Château de La Capelle, was redesigned by two gifted decorators and gardeners, Robartus Shootemeyer and Paul Hanbury. The latter was a descendant of the family that donated the gardens of Wisley to the Royal Horticultural Society, and created the magnificent hillside plantations of La Mortola in Ventimiglia, now an Italian public park. Among the several châteaux and gardens restored by this imaginative pair, Arpaillargues has become an elegant country hotel, a fate not uncommon for ancient medieval properties.

FOREIGN FASHIONS

The early Renaissance brought many changes. New models of elegance arrived from the south, but also from the French court that was itself imitating Italian fashions. It cannot be said, however, that fortifications were unnecessary in a time of bitter religious wars. One of Provence's loveliest ruins stands near Pertuis; its history bears witness to the dangers of the period. After the destruction of the nearby medieval village keep by Calvinists in 1545, the local lords moved to a fortified valley farm on this site. The next generation transformed the original property into the elegant manor house one can imagine from today's vestiges, inspired by the French court and two grander neighbors, the Tour d'Aigues and Ansouis. Besides making important architectural changes, they designed a new garden with avenues of fruit trees alternating with roses, lanes of poplars and mulberries, and formal parterres for vegetables. But all this once again fell prey to the ravages of religious struggles only a few years later. Today the ruined château sits peacefully behind squares planted with almond orchards.

When this property was still a farmstead, the texts of the time called it "la Grande

The medieval castle
of La Capelle boasts a sophisticated rock garden in its inner courtyard,
including broom, shrubby hypericums,
buddleias, chaste trees, Japanese maples, phlomis, abelias, spireas, and privet.
Floral display contrasts delicacy and fragility,
descending lines and fine texture, with the solid masses of the fortress.

Bastide." This name can still be found all over maps today in Provence, designating large farming estates. The term "bastide," which may have come from Piedmont, has long puzzled historians over the naming of lordly residences in the south. The early *castra* of tenth-century texts began to overlap already in the first half of the thirteenth with *bastida*, sometimes used interchangeably with *turris*, or tower. All medieval fortifications had towers, of course, and this new category seems at first to have had the same functions as its immediate ancestor: controlling major junctions, borders, passages and fords, uniting rural populations in the village network we know still today, constituting a symbolic affirmation of personal power. Like other castles, bastides might belong to any branch of the emerging great families or to a bishop. Very soon, however, they developed the double vocation which for most writers defines the category today: a country estate combined with a working farm.

Today, the word "bastide" applies most often to properties surrounding the cities of Aix and Marseille, which in the eighteenth century could be counted in the hundreds. These manor houses are justly famous for their fine gardens— Aix alone is cited in the *Oxford Companion to Gardens* from all of Provence. Because the regional parliament was centered in this city as of the sixteenth century, the Aix country homes

*The explosion of almond blossoms
in spring is heralded like the arrival of new wine—they are particularly striking
in front of this ruined Renaissance château (top and above).
The shaded parterre at Bargemone exhibits a particularly charming blend of
Mediterranean formality and intimacy (opposite).*

have always been in the public eye. Even recent books on Provençal gardens focus almost entirely on these properties that line rural roads like so many lordly suburbs, each with its stone pillars and wrought-iron gate. They were no doubt the first southern French domains in which house and garden were viewed as one ornamental unit, part of a common design. Life was good at the bastide—so much so, it would seem,

that northerners early on showed impatience with relaxed southern mores. An intendant of the galleys in Marseille wrote Colbert in exasperation: "You will never establish in Marseille that great and fine commercial center it should be. . . . They are so degenerate in their bastides, miserable holes of houses that they have in their countrysides, that they abandon the best business deals in the world rather than losing out on an entertainment at the bastide."

The term *pavillon* was used for those bastides that were almost suburban, closer to town and less rural in style. One of the most beautiful gardens of the Aix area belongs to the Pavillon de Bidaine. First designed as a hunting lodge for a bishop of Avignon in the early seventeenth century, it was given by Louis XIV to a chevalier whose heirs later sold it, in 1744, to a bourgeois family. Only in the twentieth century did it change hands again, when a visionary Englishman, Hubert Haincque de Saint-Senoch, restored the numerous fountains and basins of

*The Mignarde is one of the finest
remaining examples of an eighteenth-century bastide. These country
houses near Aix and Marseille possess
the best-known Provençal gardens to date (top and above).
The trees at Bargemone are useful
both for shade and wind protection (opposite).*

the original design. With the help of some of Europe's best landscapers, he planned an elaborate water garden in which double low stone walls following canals outlined baroque islands full of plantings.

With English taste, he mixed small trees, shrubs and perennials—purple-leaved plums next to tamarisks, olives and loquats, with iris, columbine, and cerastium at their feet. Not a collector's garden, this is above all designed for shape, color and texture. Stone, plants and water make a harmonious whole that can be discovered in its entirety from the terrace above and from each successive story of the house, its intimacy and mystery revealed in a walk between the canals. Statues are strategically placed under hanging foliage.

This is above all a property in which stone and water marry over and over again in extravagant show: even the overflow of its many fountains is caught and held in outer basins

that frame and maintain the display. The twentieth-century additions blend beautifully with the earlier, baroque spirit. The current owner, Lillian Williams, has added some imported Italian cypresses on upper levels, a formal entrance at the bottom of the water garden, a lavender lake in the midst of the old orchard on the garden's edges. For here, too, the elegant heart of the garden is surrounded by the agricultural geometries, a formal framework for the exuberant interior flow.

Bastide gardens offer one of the best examples of mixed foreign influences, sometimes northern, sometimes southern, absorbed into the local spirit of place and time. Their grottoes were constructed fifty years after the northern fashion, and garden sculpture was popular in eighteenth-century Provençal gardens much longer than in the Ile-de-France. Gifted local artisans created their own style and school and their harmonies, when successful, are purely Provençal. The same phenomenon can be observed all over Provence in the châteaux of the seventeenth and eighteenth centuries, where there is great variety in both architecture and garden design.

Moreover, even the specialists disagree about outside influences. The *Oxford Companion to Gardens* describes the famous Albertas garden south of Aix as "Italianate," whereas local expert Nerte Fustier-Dautier believes it was taken almost directly from northern garden treatises, calling it more Parisian than Provençal. Italian influence has been ascribed to all the most famous neoclassical gardens of the area—the bastide series as a whole, or the Jardin de la Fontaine in Nîmes, for a variety of reasons: their terracing; the solid presence of massed stone (already as retaining walls) contrasting with dark, evergreen foliage; the dramatic alternation of sun and shade; the role of individual trees of character; or the closeness of untamed nature or cultivated fields. Water, it is pointed out, is here treasured for its motion and music, or for its reflective stillness in the Italian manner; it never, as at Versailles, becomes such an important feature that it exists entirely as sculpture in its own right, masking

The carved stone balustrades
of the elegant water gardens of the Pavillon de Bidaine overlook orchards
and a lake of lavender (above and opposite).
Fountains are everywhere at Bidaine, and here contrast with
a mirror of reflecting water and the
soaring branches of plane trees (following page).

the surrounding greenery when turned on for momentary effect. Surely, however, much of this supposed Italian influence results directly from indigenous conditions. The commonly found low, broad parterres could be either French or Italian, but local topography as well as custom keeps them from attaining French scale or flatness. And as mentioned earlier, they almost always are planted with tall shade trees, which implies other pleasures than those of viewing from afar or above. How difficult to disentangle the threads of external sources from local inspiration!

This is particularly true in those domains where successive centuries have each brought improvements to both buildings and garden. Barbentane, from the late seventeenth and early eighteenth centuries, is by far the most famous château of this period in lower Provence, described as Parisian by some, as Italian by others. Still belonging to the family that built it,

it has kept its original furniture but not, however, its formal gardens, which were converted into a landscape park in the eighteenth century in spite of abrupt differences of level. The northern terraces allow a detailed appreciation of the upper branches of three-hundred-year-old oriental plane trees from above and below, grown from seeds brought back by an ambassador ancestor. Outstanding, even humorous rococo garden sculpture has survived along the upper level. The eastern parterre was replaced around 1880 with an orangery and a pool.

Where northern French influence was strongest, it shaped an attitude to the land that remains exceptional in Provence as a whole: the pleasure, as Saint-Simon put it, of "forcing nature." Southern gardens conceived in this spirit not only sever connections with the wilderness, but also rise above the utilitarian concerns of the local agricultural tradition. The parliamentarians of Aix, whose center of interest was naturally Paris, sometimes adopted this attitude in the bastide gardens. The Counts of Albertas built one of the loveliest squares in Aix in imitation of the Place Vendôme; the present count is proud that his elegant garden contains no olive trees, and cites a passage from the Prince de Ligne in which his ancestor was congratulated on this same distinction. It does, however, have orchards.

The most striking example must be the gardens at La Barben. Below the castle's medieval fortifications extends the narrow strip of seventeenth-century parterre, bordered by a trout stream, the Touloubre. Its floral embroideries, basins and statues are reputed to have been designed by Le Nôtre; they are visible from the castle windows on the promontory high above, from the flat road below, and from the ramp leading to the main gate. As one mounts the latter, one can also judge the height of the nineteenth-century sequoia and cembra pine that rise so incongruously from the very middle of the design. The formal rectangle has good rhythms and its multiple points of visual entry are a successful feature; but the wild hill beyond stands in shocking contrast to the formalities of the foreground. No extension of this

*At Bidaine, stone, plants and water
combine in a harmonious whole that can be discovered from the terrace above
and from each successive story of the house,
while its intimacy is revealed by walking between the canals (above).
Detail of the elaborate gardens of Albertas,
south of Aix, where a solitary faun keeps watch (opposite).*

garden, the *garrigue* here is intrusive and unwelcome—unless it is the garden that has been artificially and unsuccessfully grafted onto a space as unlike Le Nôtre's sites as could possibly be imagined.

"Forcing nature" in Provence can mean huge expanses of lawn requiring conspicuous consumption of water. It is not only modern owners of suburban villas who set their weeping willows in a bright patch of grass: the Popes in Avignon made it a point of honor to have an expensive greensward, watered by bucket brigades. Of course, as Edith Wharton said of Italian country gardens, a flat stretch of grass or bowling green often lay like a jewel, enclosed in box hedging or low statue-lined walls near the house. It was used for games, in Provence as in Italy, and bears little relation to the large-scale French expanse of *tapis vert*. Today lawns belong to the English model. Some of the most elaborate contemporary gardens display them lavishly, as do so many southern municipali-

ties in their beautifully planted traffic islands.

Lawns, sculpture, canals and geometric plantings of trees and hedges characterize the parks of still other French-inspired, neoclassical châteaux from the eighteenth century, particularly a group of elegant country residences for city folk known as *folies*. One such stands near Carpentras, peacefully secluded in the midst of rolling fields and back country lanes.

*The magnificent fountains
at Albertas feature superb eighteenth-century sculpture (top).
On the terraces at the Château of Barbentane,
the small-scaled rococo sculptures are particularly distinctive (above).*

*The northern terraces at Barbentane
allow close inspection of the three-hundred-year-old oriental plane trees grown
from seeds brought back by an ambassador
ancestor. In the spring, flowering Judas trees dominate the scene.*

Built mainly between 1750 and 1770, it has kept its statuary, its formal canals graced with black and white swans, and a charming little stone bridge linking the house terrace to the parterres beyond. Its finest feature is an octagonal pool that reflects a row of ancient plane trees, with an obelisk marking the main axis. This park is currently undergoing restoration, but will remain strictly private. The farmstead that stands to one side has lost part of its vegetable plot to a tennis court and swimming pool, and the main path, not visible from the house, will be a rose arbor. Olive trees have been kept in this part of the garden.

The revolutionary period inevitably brought changes and surprises. One of Provence's most ambitious and prestigious château gardens was destroyed, along with most of the building, in 1792. This was the Tour d'Aigues in the Luberon, for three centuries a model to all those around, though itself constantly redone in imitation of distant fashions. The Dukes of Les-

diguières who were its first important landscapers regularly frequented Versailles, and counted among their number a tutor of Louis XV. They built the grand northern terrace with its French parterres: colorful floral compartments separated by low box hedging, an elegant half-moon basin and avenues of poplars and elms. An extensive park was at that time enclosed in walls four meters high, which meant displacing a major highway connecting Gambois to Aix. Much the same attitude to surrounding communities was held by the Bruny family, which took over the property in 1720. They were certainly enlightened gardeners, however, who redesigned the axes of the garden asymmetrically, introducing horse chestnuts, lilacs, thuyas and planes. There was also an ornamental vegetable garden mixed with fruit trees, decorated with six basins and fountains; and a grand canal lined with elm avenues and yew topiary. The park beyond was divided into halves, one given over to orchards and vineyards,

*Forcing nature: at La Barben,
the wild hillside contrasts strikingly with the Le Nôtre garden (above).
A neoclassical folie in a
characteristic Provençal setting near Carpentras (opposite).*

while in the woods of the other side a labyrinth and an elaborate menagerie were installed.

The last baron of the Tour d'Aigues, also president of the parliament in Aix, was passionately involved in agricultural research. He introduced new varieties (such as the angora goat), developed progressive techniques, and collected plants from the four corners of the earth. He grew, for example, several sorts of jasmines and decorative solanums, which are coming back into favor among southern gardeners. Here were trees that many gardeners still show with pride: Chinese mulberries, false acacias, as well as mimosas, maples, laburnums. The baron was a great appreciator of nature and a man of considerable refinement—it seems he had his carp castrated to produce a finer flavor. He got along badly with his peasantry, however, and his estate was violently attacked, then divided into lots and sold. Some impressive ruins of the castle still remain.

Another somewhat eccentric property from the same period, this one well preserved, fortunately, is the Château de Castille, west of the Rhône. It has been much photographed, since it belonged to the art collector Douglas Cooper, whose friend Picasso did a set of erotic frescoes along the east terrace (outlines made with small dark pebbles on a white wall). What is most striking about Castille, however, is its columns. They are everywhere, enhancing a bastide-like central building—the classic rectangle with four corner towers—with their rows all along the lower story and balustrade edging the roof. The extensions still retain the colonnade along the driveway and parts of the great stretch that imitated Saint Peter's in Rome. The vast park was once full of *fabriques* that also involved pillars in various proportions—one still stands, though in ruins, across the public road in a grove of cypresses. A temple inside the château was inspired by the famous ones at Paestum.

The man responsible for these marvels, the celebrated Baron de Castille, had much admired the antiquities in Italy. Work was carried out between 1785 and 1815, in spite of the Revolution. Indeed, local historian Hervé Aliquot suggests that the design and decor of this elaborate property owed much to the ceremonies of freemasonry. Today, the garden has kept wonderful boxwood labyrinths on both sides of the now rounded façade, the lines of the vegetation continuing those of the building. Needless to say, these are planted with shade trees, but also roses in the conversation circles. There are many softening details like the trumpet vine climbing one corner of the house, and the basin set against the wood beyond. The park that still extends north of the château offers the typical mixture of holm oak and pines with box and other low-growing evergreens, and contains Romantic tombs of the baron's family.

Some properties from the early 1800s have clung to the preceding century in a manner that combines the charms of both periods. The Château du Martinet was rebuilt on the same site after its destruction by local revolutionaries. Its ivy-covered courtyard walls were built from stones available when the ramparts of Carpentras were torn down in 1814. Still neoclassical in style, this castle's plan shows its function as a summer residence. The *cour d'honneur* faces north, around a charming santolina-edged basin. Beyond its gate extends a fine park full of parasol pines, green and white oaks, laurustinus and box, where one corner shelters a truffle orchard. The three spokes of its half-wheel design each lead to a striking mountain view, now visible only in winter. Connecting these open axes are many winding paths, conversation circles around urns, shaded benches. The approaches to the house itself have been made more formal with hedges,

At the Château de Castille,
columns abound, their rows transforming a classic Provence bastide
into an Italianate folie *(above and opposite).*

çal type of domain that is not so much a fortress or a bastide (though there may be a tower or turret), still less a French neoclassical *folie* (though there may be good sculptural detailing), but rather a large and lordly farmstead. There are still, of course, always two residences: a stately one for the owners and another, off to one side, for the overseer. But the main building has kept the long, rectangular shape of simpler *mas* with smaller cubes and rectangles added on. This style may be the most truly indigenous, descending even more directly, perhaps, from the Roman estates that so proudly proclaimed their agricultural vocation. These châteaux no longer shine with marble, but they have their own elegance.

sculpted boxwood balls and a newly planted cypress avenue. The château's southern aspect gives onto hayfields, though a small picturesque lake planted with rare bald cypresses lies near the old vegetable garden.

Romantic "English" gardens served as a model for many nineteenth-century transformations, with varying success. Fonscolomb also lost its original park but kept its sculpture, and gained a game reserve, a charming pond, and winding, wooded walks. The two-tiered hillside park of the Château d'Aramon has Mediterranean versions of English landscaping, classified as such by the Caisse Nationale des Monuments Historiques. The woodland paths of the upper garden lead through copses of almond and olive trees, hackberries, cypresses, parasol pines, bupleurums and laurustinus that grow so well in this lime-intense soil; in spite of a buried cistern in its midst, however, it gets very dry in summer. The topsoil is so sparse that the original plantation holes were sometimes made with dynamite. The later, lower park (linked by a bridge to the upper one in 1858) has more soil and more water. Here roses and fruit trees were planted, as well as palm and bamboo from, of course, the extensive collections at Prafrance, which served as a model and a source for so many nineteenth-century château gardens. It is currently being transformed once again.

Such is the rather considerable range of châteaux and gardens that took inspiration from foreign models, both northern and southern. Many other examples could be cited. But there exists another, more specifically Proven-

VINEYARD AND FARMYARD CHÂTEAUX

Properties of this type differ from more modest farmsteads in several important ways: they may

The park and architecture of the Château de Castille owe much to the esoteric symbolism of the Revolutionary period.

be sited on a slight rise to dominate the surrounding land, whether or not water is readily available nearby. (Builders were always confident that water could be piped in from some far-off piece of land purchased for that purpose.) The formal entrance may face north rather than south or southeast, if the owners first came primarily in summer. The house façade and terrace make an open unit that is not disturbed by an arbor or shade trees in front of the building. This space often includes two levels: the terrace immediately in front and a second one below, also flattened, which may have a parterre or a reflecting pool where a *mas* would have only a well. Instead of a low wall, a stone or wrought-iron balustrade may separate these two spaces, and there will be Anduze jars for decoration. There may also be extensive use of garden sculpture throughout. The outer edges may still include a greater or lesser expanse of eighteenth or nineteenth-century parkland, with majestic pines and oaks

underplanted with box or laurel hedging that may still be, when labor is available, pruned into rounded shapes to set off the wildness of the nearby wood. Any or all of these features may confer a nobler status on a prosperous farm (and in many cases were added when owners were ennobled). But in spite of these distinctions, the architecture and general mood respond to an agricultural vocation, providing a characteristic southern blend.

Alphonse Daudet appreciated this mix at the Château de Montauban, where he stayed while writing his popular *Letters from My Mill*. He admired "a strange old dwelling that starts as a château with its flights of steps, its terrace colonnaded in the Italian style, and that finishes with farmhouse walls, perches for peacocks, vines over the doorway, a fig tree twining itself around the iron well-head, sheds glittering with harrows and ploughshares. . . ." But like Lawrence Durrell, he prefers picturesque decrepitude to robust activity.

The northern courtyard of the
Château du Martinet blends green and gray santolina around a central
basin, always an effective combination (above).
Many fine domains in Provence are like larger, grander versions
of the great farms of landed gentry.
The imposing façade of the Domaine de Brantes is reflected
in a T-shaped pool (following page).

In some cases, a farm that ancestors proudly refined into a château has now become primarily an agricultural exploitation once more. This is the case with an estate near Goult, a rectangular manor house with Renaissance detailing around the windows and a stately gate leading to no less than three separate courtyards where old roses grow up half-stuccoed walls. It has even kept vestiges of its original *tèse*. But all

this is a bit abandoned, whereas beyond, in the modern greenhouses, hundreds of tiny melon and tomato plants await planting out in early spring.

Another stately property, on a terraced hillside, has kept a vast vegetable garden below the house, backed by a fine cut-stone wall with balustrade. Once planted with olive orchards and vines, the slope on which this estate is situated was transformed into a chic suburb in the 1930s and now shelters many of the town's most exclusive ornamental gardens. But this domain, which predated this caprice, has retained its authentic farmstead character and its elegant façade supporting one of the most magnificent trellises in Provence.

Other old estates have severed ties with agriculture, sometimes lying too close to modern cities to retain much land. The Domaine de Brantes, dating from the seventeenth, eighteenth and nineteenth centuries, has become a private enclave in the midst of a modern industrial

*A stately Rhône valley
property set on a terraced hillside has been maintained in the old style.
Its ancient hackberry and magnificent,
wisteria-laden trellis shade the façade, while its fine stone balustrade overlooks
an extensive vegetable garden.*

145

suburb, protected still by a veritable forest of plane trees. The Countess de Brantes and her late husband established elegant formal gardens around a T-shaped basin that echoes and reflects the long rectangle of the façade. Sculpted box at various heights gives further structure, under the canopy of a particularly magnificent *Magnolia grandiflora*.

Many other châteaux actively combine past prestige and current production, however, particularly of wines. Château Bas, between Aix and the Durance, has kept its formal parterres, its flower-decked well, its giant horse chestnuts that rise to match turrets decked with multicolored tiles, although the gardens now include a swimming pool. In the "wild garden" beyond the formal gate, on a grassy, sloping wildflower meadow, sits a Roman temple fragment backed by a twelfth-century apse. This amazing "garden sculpture," a focal point from the château and also a place from which to view the parterres, impresses far more than any strategic-

ally placed neoclassical temple could ever do.

The Château de Bellecoste in the Gard carries on tradition in the heart of a modern enterprise. It was built as a summer home for an aristocratic family from Nîmes, and thus was situated not only near a spring but on a rise of land that would deliberately catch the wind. And indeed, the sea breeze in summer comes along daily around three in the afternoon. Unfortunately, the mistral also pays its visits: on October 6, 1961, its gusts knocked down ten parasol pines of considerable size, and over four hundred holm oaks.

This is a property with its roots deep in Provençal history: one of the heroes of the Camargue, Folco de Baroncelli, spent his early childhood here. Not too much has changed since his time, tornadoes notwithstanding. The domain is still surrounded by copses of wild local trees: oaks and pines, but also laurustinus and bay laurels, and some wild phillyreas.

Bellecoste, which is open to the public and

*The Domaine de Brantes
is surrounded by a forest of plane trees that protect it from the encroaching city,
but create mountains of unwanted leaves in the fall.*

can even be rented for weddings, gives some idea of what an old-fashioned working farm was like. Three cypresses stand by the driveway at the west end of the property, representing, according to local custom, food, a place to sleep and friendship. The original summer residence faces northwest in a horseshoe shape, with a chapel sheltered by the wings. A raised terrace along this façade has a modest grouping of laurels,

Judas trees and irises. It faces a large sloping lawn with a fountain that provides the perfect setting every spring for a well-attended plant fair. Professionals and amateurs come here from all over the south to sell and exchange rare perennials.

The enclosed farmyard lies to the southeast. Visitors enter through a gate, pass chickens, goats and pigeons and high-stacked firewood, to purchase the products of the *terroir*: the current owners sell their own wine, and also honey, preserves, olive oil and even *foie gras*. Vineyards and ten acres of olive trees lie farther on. There are more than two hundred acres in all.

If instead of turning west into the farmyard, visitors continue south through mixed shrubbery toward a high-walled garden, they will find themselves in the old *potager*, now the present owner's private domain. Its southern boundary gives onto open fields without a wall. This space is truly a delight for all the senses. It contains

The iron fence at Brantes supports
a particularly elegant wisteria (top). The inner gardens at Château Bas can be
glimpsed from the Roman temple site outside.
The TGV, the new fast train, threatens this and many other equally
fine properties in the area (above).
The eighteenth-century Château de la Nerthe at Châteauneuf-du-Pape is beautifully
set off by its surrounding vineyards (following page).

an indescribable entanglement of vegetables, cherry, quince and apricot trees, long rows of irises (a famous collection of more than four hundred varieties), a greenhouse and shed with layer after layer of potted sedums and sempervivums, protected by a row of red-leaved hazelnut bushes. There are very few roses, and these are chosen only for their fragrance. Even the vegetables are exceptional: red-ribbed chard, snow peas with a fine purple bloom. It is a paradise that takes time and curiosity to explore, and it does not easily display its riches to those for whom order is the first quality of a garden.

This example is not unique and, although each has its own character and harmony, there are many such farm-châteaux in the region. There is a timelessness about this kind of setting. One thinks of Durrell's interview with an elderly count, living among his vineyards, dispensing "warm hospitality beside his own quiet lily pond, seated under a shady pergola of vine and plumbago." Durrell, of course, appreciated country manor houses above all for their "romantic melancholy of desuetude." But many of these properties were transformed during the golden years of the mid-nineteenth century by owners who wanted to improve their land and their lot, to benefit from the progress of their time, to maintain a position in the forefront both of fashion and commercial enterprise.

A local writer, Elizabeth Barbier, described an entire dynasty of such Provençal landowners in her serial novel, *Les Gens de Mogador*. In the 1860s, a young married couple take in hand

his family château in the Alpilles. The husband spends his time managing the estate's agricultural production and the community that participates therein. The wife's concerns are raising a family and running a household that can shine among the other landed gentry of the neighborhood. Together they plan the pleasure garden. Overgrown plane trees are removed to let light onto the façade, where a round pond is set in the lawn, edged with a hazelnut hedge and enhanced by an old Lebanese cedar. A new, March-flowering magnolia honors Julia's birthday, and beyond this sunny space, laurustinus are pruned to make a formal conversation circle around a stone bench. There are flower borders and a rose garden.

Above all, Julia's husband creates an avenue of alternating palms and orange trees in front of the house, the former planted directly in the ground, the latter in Anduze jars. Julia remembers the old-fashioned manor house that was her childhood home, with its traditional wisteria trellis and shade trees, its hydrangeas and flowering urns along the southern terrace, and takes pride in her château's new elegance. This garden will serve as the stage for elaborate fêtes on warm summer evenings. Its landscaping is simple, but combines refinement and comfort, pleasure and profit. The property that inspired this novel, called Estoublon, today sells its wine and olive oil to the public in the old farmyard.

This portrait illustrates once more the rich texture of traditional country life in Provence. If this version of "the good life" resembles the

Ancient populations once worshiped Hercules at the Château de Servane in Mouriès. It too resembles a noble farmhouse, its gentrification confirmed by the stone dovecote that greets visitors under the canopy of planes beside the canal.

one already evoked for the farmstead, it is no coincidence: the Provençal château is still at heart one great exalted farm. The designs of Provence, once freed from their medieval battlements, through centuries of enlightened dialogue with northern and southern models, have never forsaken their original Roman inspiration. They are now, as then, rooted in the land itself.

The young hero and heroine of Elizabeth Barbier's novel, Les Gens de Mogador, *restored this park in the nineteenth century. Today the Château d'Estoublon, which inspired this fiction, still sells its farm produce, olive oil and wine on the premises.*

THE CITY
STAGE

While the countryside of Provence has attained the status of myth and model far and wide, southern French cities are largely taken for granted. Yet their importance is tremendous, not least for the development of the landscape. Dating often from Greek trading posts or the earliest Celtic *oppida*, towns like Nîmes, Arles, and Avignon became Roman metropolises; they kept their identities through the darkest ages, never wholly disappearing (thanks in some cases to their role in church administration), emerging in the twelfth century as powerful and remarkably independent city-states—much like their Italian neighbors. These commercial and religious centers maintained their authority throughout the centuries by controlling much of the best agricultural resources. They afforded protection to surrounding rural populations and the latter, in turn, fed the cities, though not always willingly. Problems arise today because the great postwar expansion has led to the building up some of the area's most fertile and best-irrigated farmland.

The Mediterranean connection kept these communities active even when trade in the north had ground to a halt. Each of these small inland cities occupies a strategic site at a river junction or a mountain route that leads toward the sea. The Roman general Marius had his idle soldiers build a canal to link the marshy hamlet of the Arlate tribe to the coast, thus establishing the fortunes of Arles. Avignon sits at the confluence of the Rhône and the Durance, dominating these vigorous currents from the heights of a natural rock fortress, the Rocher des Doms. The Rhône was both artery and boundary in medieval times, so much so that its boatmen said, instead of port and starboard, "empire" for the left bank and "kingdom" for the right.

These cities may have reached forty or fifty thousand inhabitants in Roman times, then shrunk to a tenth of that size before gradually expanding again in the later Middle Ages. In 1149, Avignon received its charter of freedom guaranteeing its right to self-government in the form of a town council composed half of nobility and half of merchants. This privilege was extraordinary for the time, but was soon a commonplace in the region. The "consuls" who managed these communities were echoing Roman practice, however distant. Some town councilors descended from the "urban knights," vassals of more powerful lords who had given them the charge of defending the walled townships. Taking their names from nearby hamlets such as Boulbon and Laurade, they received land for their services, and built country castles near the cities they were bound to protect. Thus began the urban oligarchies so famous in the south. At the same time, professions such as law, money-changing, and textile and weapons manufacture produced a wealthy middle class that also invested in the land, with a view to future ennoblement. City administrations also owned land—Avignon once held title to the entire Comtat Venaissin. They may not have been kind landlords: when Louis VIII won his siege of this city in 1226 and ordered its ramparts dismantled, it seems that the local peasantry lent a willing hand.

Today these larger cities and the smaller market towns have kept their almond-shaped kernel of medieval streets, full of folds like leaves ready to open, enclosed not by ramparts but by encircling boulevards that have replaced, for the most part, the city walls. Always the name "Rue des Lices" conjures up the ghost of medieval battlements, evoking the open spaces just within where knights could practice their jousting. Market gardens and vineyards were located here as well. Some walls still stand—Avignon's are famous worldwide; but Arles, Nîmes, Tarascon and a multitude of smaller communities still have impressive medieval portals.

Such cities impress by the sheer quantity of their mineral presence—Austrian novelist Joseph Roth said of Avignon that "it is a garden of stone full of stone flowers." Their islands of greenery, public and private, are ringed with walls, rich with ruins and sculpture, more concentrated than in the grand parks of châteaux, more polished and refined, for the most part, than in the rustic constructions of village

In the public Jardins des Doms in Avignon, "a voluptuous, romantic nymph in the middle of the sluggish green water is still dancing on her pedestal" (South African novelist André Brink).

behind the Roman theater stands, where yet another castle relic presides over some thirteen acres of Mediterranean vegetation.

But even the smaller-proportioned private town courtyards lend themselves to theatrical display more than their village equivalents. Their centers are broader and more formal, their upper levels wider and flatter, allowing multiple viewpoints from which to see the show. And show there is, for although these green enclaves are hidden from the outside world behind high walls, they have been carefully designed for their own actors and audiences.

PUBLIC PERFORMANCE

Each of the Rhône cities possesses its own strong character, bearing the mark of its particular history. Avignon today is still "the papal city": the arrival of popes, cardinals and their retinues in the early fourteenth century increased the population from about 6,000 to 40,000—one historian's "modest" estimate—and caused a housing crisis. Whole city blocks were confiscated by cardinals to be rebuilt as palaces—thirty or fifty houses at a time. Evicted owners used indemnities to rebuild on the outskirts, on land reclaimed from the Rhône. This land was already partly occupied by mills, monasteries, vineyards and houses with gardens, now guaranteed tax-exempt and immune from confiscation. This area was enclosed in the present city walls some years later, when marauders from the Hundred Years War ravaged the countryside.

The fourteenth-century city was dominated, like Avignon today, by the Palais des Papes (Pope's Palace), erected in a twenty-year period and deemed by the chronicler Froissart "the finest house in Europe." Cardinals' residences (or *livrées*, as they became known) imitated the great model in that they too included one or two inside courtyards or cloisters. Towers were of prime necessity, for here as in the country bastides (the term was also used for the country houses of these prelates), turrets symbolized power. Today, the great Livrée Ceccano has become Avignon's public library. Its first-story

courtyards. Inhabitants today struggle to reconcile the demands of modern life with these sometimes proud, sometimes awkward vestiges of the past; some ruins are famous public landmarks, others give character to private dwellings, still others encumber, like the Templar chapel that long had to serve as laundry room for a modest Avignon hotel. City space is so precious that any choice to preserve or change it can have momentous consequences, both for buildings and gardens, and city gardens more than any others are inseparable from the surrounding architecture.

Within this mineral universe, some gardens are designed with a view to historical authenticity, others become the theater of original new productions. Indeed, the architectural skeleton of a southern city garden can inspire particularly dramatic settings—sometimes by their very scale, which may involve entire mountains, rivers and canals, splendid vistas. Public gardens invariably incorporate imposing ruins: the city center of Vaison-la-Romaine is a park built around spectacular Roman digs that can be viewed on several levels, and even include a theater. Beaucaire's castle, which was dismantled by order of Richelieu, was surrounded by a "wild, tangled garden covering the side of the hill . . . a garden without flowers, with little steep, rough paths that wind under a plantation of small, scrub stone-pines." So spoke Henry James, who admired the benches and the view, and concluded that "a sweet desolation, an everlasting peace, seemed to hang in the air." Orange has a view of the hill of Saint-Eutrope

*At the Jardins des Doms,
the ramps leading to the summit were inspired by Italian gardens, while the
garden itself imitated English and Parisian models (above).
A fourteenth-century cloister, a nineteenth-century botanical garden for
Avignon's doctors, and today a completely new
conception for the Square Agricole Perdiguier. The metal arches will
support a collection of climbing plants (opposite).*

reading room has restored period ceilings, and its proud tower, which once contained an important Jesuit observatory, still looms high. Its garden, a small but gracious plot curving along a city street, is planted only with trees and shrubs that were in use in the fourteenth century.

The Pope's Palace still stands in splendor, though few writers like it: Durrell condemns it as "hideous packing-cases of an uncouth ugliness." It is the second most-visited monument in France outside of Paris, as well as a modern convention center. Plans are afoot to restore its gardens; and parts of the orchards of Urban V, which stretched along its east flank, already offer shady repose to weary travelers. The account books of the palace provide the best information on the gardens as well as the artistic activity at court: they record the pruning of trees, the cleaning of a well. . . . Huge quantities of earth were moved to provide good soil in the right places on the upper levels, and there was

that most precious of southern garden features, a heavily watered lawn. Clement VI (who bragged that his predecessors did not know how to be pope) added a fountain with griffons and more floral groupings. The popes did not disdain arbors, it seems, and Urban V (the most devout of the Avignon popes) was proud of his "Galeria Roma." Trellising with vines provided shade in many places. Vegetables mixed with flowers even in these august premises, squares of green and white cabbage, fennel, sage, borage, violets and roses, with marjoram borders. The term *parare* occurs frequently in the texts describing these gardens, stressing appearance but also careful arrangement. And yet the style must have been intimate: paths were small and winding, simple *carriere* meant to allow his Holiness passage among the plantations. This combination of intimacy and elegance will soon be visible again, thanks to current restoration work.

Avignon's best-loved public park lies just

*The city of Avignon presents
a handsome silhouette. The towers of the Pope's Palace dominate the cool greenery
of the Jardins des Doms, set on the city's most ancient site.*

above the Pope's Palace, on the summit of the Rocher des Doms. This pinnacle, a solid cliff dominating the river, successively supported a Neolithic settlement, a Roman army camp and the first castle of the counts of Provence. It has thus been the heart of the town and its main defense since prehistoric times. In the twelfth century, the bishop's palace on the Rocher stood opposite the castle, composed of four buildings around a greensward. Between the two small, extended fields and houses with gardens, the former was given the name *champeaux*, a term that is still used for the main entrance to the nearby Pope's Palace. There were two quarries on the Rocher at that time. The castle was destroyed by lightning in 1650, but the quarries and mills survived. In the eighteenth century this space, like the *allées* outside the ramparts, became popular for elegant promenades.

After the Revolution the area was slowly transformed. Charitable associations hired unemployed workers for the initial restructuring, and a mayor of Avignon who proudly claimed Napolean III as his patron and advisor in city planning had the gardens of the Doms laid out as they are today. Their winding approaches were treated in the Italian style, the summit as a *jardin anglais*. The grotto and rockery were Parisian, constructed on special order by Combos, a rock specialist who had worked on promenades in the capital.

Most writers visiting Avignon since its creation have commented on this park. Henry James admired its "thick, dark foliage" and said it reminded him "faintly and a trifle perversely" of the Pincian gardens in Rome. Michel Tournier visited Avignon as the internationally renowned summer theater festival was closing down, when (as he says), the hippies stop sleeping in the streets to join their parents on the tennis courts of Deauville and Biarritz. In the gardens he witnessed one last dramatic spectacle, a woman alone, heavily made up, gesticulating for a hidden audience—a man out of sight in the city jail below the wall. At times one can find a whole chorus of prisoners' girlfriends by the balustrade, a poignant spectacle that will continue until the prison is replaced by the restored Papal gardens on the Rue Banasterie.

The Rocher des Doms has kept its Second Empire layout and atmosphere. A large circular pond lies half-shaded by tall trees, with "a voluptuous, romantic nymph in the middle of the sluggish green water still dancing on her pedestal" (so noted South African novelist André Brink). Swans glide by, bright café umbrellas decorate one side. The rockery, somewhat comical in its disproportion to the massive mountain on which it stands, provides climbing for children and a grotto whose fakery is part of its charm. Regimented roses line lawns, and evergreen shrub groupings direct the *promeneur* to shaded benches. Closer to the edge, the garden takes on a more precise character, due to vantage points on several levels that reveal "on three sides . . . the loops and curls of the Rhône carving out the embankments of its bed in the carious limestone, sculpting the soft flanks of the nether hills" (Durrell). It is not just the view that impresses, but the steepness, the leveling of the garden's boundaries in small, intimate olive groves, elsewhere in broad expanses of stone with elegant balustrades. The Jardin des Doms is both intimate and dignified, as well as solid and comfortable, and has, like all nineteenth-century Provençal gardens of any importance, some fine specimen trees—a weeping sophora and the obligatory bamboos. Its plantations provide color in all seasons, backed by the strength of unobtrusive evergreen foliage.

Arles is one-third the size of Avignon, though for centuries in Roman and medieval times, it was a capital—at one point even a kingdom. Today it has a special small-town atmosphere that most visitors love, whether they come for the photography festival, the echoes of Van Gogh, the Roman monuments or the bullfights. For this city has remained the gateway to the Camargue, that flat, sandy delta of rice paddies, rare wildlife and huge, whitewashed ranches that contrasts so strikingly with these landscapes, though only a few kilometers distant.

The traces of Van Gogh in Arles bear surprising witness to an unexpected aspect of old city

gardens—an abundance of bright summer flowers. The painter created his garden series, often depicting public park motifs, from July to October of 1888. His first subject was a private garden, however, a plot that he described in a letter to his sister as comprising bright strips of color; poppies, marigolds, scabiosas and sunflowers. The garden of the bathing establishment also appealed to him, with its tight bed of sunflowers and its carefully aligned pots. Another letter evokes the "orange, yellow, red splashes of the flowers" which, he exclaimed to his brother, "take on an amazing brilliance, and in the limpid air there is something or other happier, more lovely than in the north. It vibrates like the bouquet by Monticelli which you have. I reproach myself for not painting flowers here." This omission would soon be corrected with a still life of oleanders and then, of course, with his series of sunflowers.

The hospital garden that Van Gogh sadly became familiar with in the fall of 1888 was also brightly decorated with rectangular beds around a circular pond, with yuccas and sculpted boxwood for structure, bedding plants and oleanders for constantly changing bloom. Now housing the cultural center Espace Van Gogh, the hospital and its gardens have been restored to correspond to Van Gogh's painting of the originals.

The Poet's Garden series that Van Gogh painted through the summer of 1888 was largely inspired by the public park near the painter's beloved "yellow house" on the Place Lamartine (destroyed by Allied bombing, along with the nearby train station, in 1944). Local tradition nonetheless situates some canvases in the still-popular Boulevard des Lices garden on the south side of town. Today it contains a bust of the painter. Certainly it resembles the paintings, with its "clipped shrubs and a weeping tree, and in the background some clumps of oleanders. And the lawn just cut with long trails of hay drying in the sun. . . . " It could well have been

The bright Jardin des Lices in Arles
resembles the public gardens that inspired Van Gogh.

the subject of Van Gogh's final garden canvas in Arles, with its lovers promenading under a large evergreen canopy "brightened by beds of geraniums, orange in the distance under the black branches." Flowers were everywhere, it would seem, in 1888. Although for this painter foliage was equally brilliant: "The bush is green, touched a little with bronze and various other tints. The grass is bright, bright green, malachite touched

with citron. . . . " This bush, still part of the public garden, provided a motif that attracted Van Gogh more than any other single natural form during his stay in Arles.

Today, the Jardin des Lices still makes excellent use of geometrically arranged bedding plants that change with the seasons. On the sloping lawn, red berberis, iris, and *Senecio cineraria* encircle beds of bright begonias, while ageratum surrounds tall yellow marigolds. Enormous cedars dominate the somewhat spotty composition, overshadowing here a group of three slight birches, there an old yew full of berries. Rocks and box hedging mark paths and transitions. And while all this is counter to current fashion, it is charmingly appropriate for the style of this garden, and for a town in which the spirits of Van Gogh and Frédéric Mistral still seem to linger (perhaps at neighboring café tables in the Place du Forum, although unknown to each other. . . .)

Van Gogh never painted the Lice garden's

Enormous cedars in the Jardin des Lices in Arles provide welcome shade against the backdrop of the ruined Roman theater.

most original feature: the Roman theater fragments that serve as its backdrop. (Similarly, in the monastery-hospital at Saint-Rémy, he avoided the Roman arch and cenotaph at his doorstep.) Today the theater has a separate entrance, and its stage is used for festival activities; but it is still surrounded by odd slabs and pillars lying picturesquely on the grass under graceful canopies of giant hackberries. Rooks, pigeons and cats love this site, itself one great sculpture garden. Wisteria decks one tall backdrop, and puffy white *Polygonum aubertii* twines along the wall that separates the theater from the street. Henry James jumped over this barrier to visit the theater by moonlight and judged it "one of the sweetest legacies of the ancient world."

Arles has of course many other gardens, courtyards with pear trees, roses, fuchsias and fragments of Roman columns, fountains surrounded by pale hibiscus, formal suspended gardens with tall cypresses tucked behind Romanesque buttressing. Beautiful wrought-iron entrance gates often allow the leisurely stroller a glimpse of private spaces. Tourists can stay in many Arlesian hotels with lovely courtyards, even parks; and the Réattu Museum has such protected spaces that visitors can inspect a flourishing carob tree. Palms thrive in a corner, protected by majestic horse chestnuts. This is a city which, because of its small scale and its ancient history, deserves the *flaneur*'s careful attention. Everywhere are vestiges of the past, carefully and comfortably built into the texture of modern life.

Many Provençal public gardens are built

around ruins, but the Jardin de la Fontaine in Nîmes is perhaps the most spectacular of them all. A sacred Roman spring and much of its surrounding architecture are incorporated into an elaborate eighteenth-century composition. Inspired by private château gardens, this was the first constructed for public use, and the first to demonstrate a real interest in antiquity. The ancient spring at its heart, lying at the foot of Mont Cavalier, was celebrated in Celtic times, and cured Augustus on his return from Spain to Rome in 24 B.C. Its shrine was among the most famous and elegant of the Roman world, turning Nîmes into the equivalent of Lourdes and Baden-Baden combined. Neglected in the Middle Ages when it lay outside the town walls, its waters muddied but still serviceable enough for mills and a Benedictine convent, it attracted city interest again in the early eighteenth century. Then a fast-growing population, an expanding textile industry, a drought, the dangers of plague from its polluted waters, and a new interest in the Roman vestiges all made rehabilitation of the spring desirable. In 1740, Louis XV asked his director of fortifications for the Languedoc region, J. P. Mareschal, to choose among the proposed plans for the site.

Interestingly, this garden built for the glory of a French monarch and under his distant eye has been variously called rococo and baroque, French and Italian. The site itself offers something for everyone: a steep hillside with dramatic terracing crowned by an octagonal Celtic watchtower (the famous Tour Magne); below this, broad formal expanses with lanes of shade trees (hackberries, horse chestnuts, lindens) are traversed by a canal that provides a major axis (albeit not symmetrical) and wide vistas onto the city boulevards beyond. These two worlds—vertical and horizontal—are joined by the garden's most dramatic feature, a complex series of monumental steps and levels that incorporate parts of the original Roman baths.

Today, this very public, even showy garden means many things to many people—a measure of its great success. Colette spent a quiet, contemplative moment in her "Elysian refuge,

The Jardin de la Fontaine in Nîmes: during the eighteenth-century remodeling of this Roman site, many stone benches, urns, cupids, and balustrades were purchased from a nearby château, while others were ordered from French sculptors (above). The Temple of Diana in Nîmes, where Colette took refuge on her travels (opposite). One of the first great public gardens and a successful blend of Roman and rococo, the Jardin de la Fontaine awaits further transformations, mostly on the upper levels (following page).

the Gardens of the Fountain," and said, "It is so fairy-like in this place, where the spring hangs motionless over all things. . . . Amorously, my hand caresses the warm stone of the ruined temple and the varnished leaves of the spindle-trees, which seem damp. The baths of Diana, over which I lean, still, as always, reflect Judas trees, the terebinths, the pines, the paulownias with their mauve flowers and the double purple thorns. A whole garden of reflections is spread out there below me, turning, as it decomposes in the aquamarine water, dark blue, the violet of a bruised peach, and the maroon of dried blood. Oh beautiful garden and beautiful silence, where the only sound is the muted plashing of the green, imperious water, transparent and dark, blue and brilliant as a bright dragon."

She was right: this spring had its water monster, like others in the area. When the Romans arrived and the Egyptian veterans settled in the area, the local dragon merged with an imported crocodile (symbol of the Roman legionaries) to become Nemausus, whence the city's name and the beast that still decorates its coat of arms. The upper slopes of the park sport a topiary crocodile marking the spot where the Roman theater was buried by the eighteenth-century designers (much to the horror of archaeologist Winckelman). Today, plans are afoot to uncover it.

Water dominates this garden: here too, it is sometimes peaceful and reflective, sometimes hurried and cascading.

Since the spring—and the entire city—lie where the limestone *garrigue* meets the fertile coastal plain, the fountain water emerges abruptly after seeping through a long valley of shallow limestone, where the latter is stopped by heavy clay. The Romans' marble structures were designed to cope with enormous output. Nonetheless, October 1988 will long be remembered for its flash flooding—even the sophisticated Roman engineering could not contain the

A flat stretch of parkland
leads toward the center of Nîmes; recent olive plantations on the steep hill above
were inspired by farmstead gardens.

flow both from underground and from the heavens. Cars were upended amid the rococo urns, and a dramatic rescue was effected on national television. . . . In times of drought, on the other hand, the Roman foundations may stand completely bared.

Descriptions of this garden, emphasizing its layers of history and formal elegance, often overlook its complementary wildness. Bedding plants sit in bright formal arrangements amid *garrigue* vegetation—*Quercus ilex*, box, bupleurum, amelanchiers, chaste trees, hackberries and parasol pines. This is not a collector's garden but a collection of the area's most characteristic essences. In the same manner, the elegant balustrades are flanked by outcroppings of natural rock. Whatever its French and Italian references, this is very much a Provençal garden, and it is experienced that way by the townspeople, regardless of tourist presence. Its promenades are often filled with mothers with prams, elderly strollers, or *boules* tournaments overflowing from their usual secluded space on the gardens' eastern border. Shade trees are pruned to overhang stone benches that are not too hard, it seems, for a siesta . . . and lawns may be walked on here. It is a park for all seasons, with pools of winter sunlight, good protection in uncertain spring weather from wind and sudden showers, deep summer shade and fragrance, glorious autumn color.

The city is proud of its gardens, and since Nîmes is one of Europe's most avant-garde cities architecturally, major transformations are in store. Architect Pierre Morel and landscaper Michel Corajoud plan to reconcile the work of previous designers and to some degree establish the balance that was never achieved (funds ran out on the eighteenth-century project). The ancient spring will remain the center of this water garden. But its flow will become circular, directed back up the hillside. From the Temple of Diana to the Celtic watchtower on the summit will be built a *noria*, or inverse waterfall, a gravity-defying cascade that will make water an even more spectacular central feature. Three terraces will flank this axis, planted with orange trees, a vineyard and olive plantation, all irrigated from the canal as it passes. In this manner this elegant, château-inspired garden will incorporate and acknowledge its agricultural sources. The designers plan to make this park a compendium of the region's landscape and garden variants: microclimates typical of the area will be included, a wood of green oaks, a farmstead garden (Jardin de Mazet), an olive orchard, an expanse of *garrigue*, a long vine-clad arbor.

This broad reference in space has its counterpart in time: the *noria* will extend upward the stone lines of the lower garden, but will also be a long walk through the city's history. The Temple of Diana, the future archaeological museum, vestiges of the Celtic Volcae tribe and their tower will gradually be revealed on an elongated transversal axis, making these gardens "the greatest open-air museum in Europe."

On a much smaller scale, Saint-Rémy-de-Provence has always been known as a "garden" city. This refers more to vegetable than to flower production, however. The parents of the poet Roumanille, teacher and comrade of Mistral during the nineteenth-century revival movement, were market gardeners, and their son was known as the "Poet of the Garden" just as Mistral held the title "Poet of the Farm." It is hard to imagine anything more decorative than the Saint-Rémy farmers' market, unless it is the procession of produce and flower-laden donkeys that still parade through town on feast days. The aristocratic residences of this ancient settlement hide many discreet courtyards—notably

These marble half-moons
in the Jardin de la Fontaine remain from the Roman basin at which the Emperor
Augustus took the waters and was cured (above).
The cloister garden of Saint-Paul-de-Mausole in Saint-Rémy, neglected
in Van Gogh's time, today features an ever-changing
scenario of climbing roses and plumbago, sometimes brightened with red canna
lilies edged with aspidistra in pots (opposite).

the Hôtel de l'Estrinne (now a Van Gogh center), with its quiet, simply planted inner courtyard. Marie Gasquet, a local writer, eloquently
praises Saint-Rémy: "Old townhouses, ornate
as caskets, evoke Nostradamus and the Renaissance; and the wind that blows in from the
Alpilles, where it has caressed Roman monuments, brings with it an ancient aroma of
strength and serenity. With its antiquities gilded
by the light, its houses full of life spilling into
the street; with its delicate bell tower, its
orchards, its quarries and its rich gardens,
Saint-Rémy, protected by the lion of Arles, lies
at the foot of its hills, overlooking the plain
which flows toward Avignon. . . . Here it is,
beyond doubt, in these few leagues of perfumed
earth, that the best of the Provençal heart
beats."

One of the most visited gardens in Provence
lies just at the edge of town, a stone's throw
from the Roman arch and cenotaph. This is the
former Benedictine monastery Saint-Paul-de-
Mausole, which became a hospital in the early
nineteenth century. This was the mental institu-
tion to which Van Gogh committed himself
toward the end of his life. Its twelfth-century
cloister provided him with yet another subject,
but its plantings were sadly neglected at the
time. Today the cloister is neither deserted nor
unkempt. Approached by its long, peaceful
lane, it contains an ever-changing garden full of
climbing roses and plumbago, sometimes brightened with red canna lilies edged with aspidistra
in pots.

The most ambitious garden city in Provence
today is surely Tarascon, a small, lively community on the Rhône between Avignon and Arles.
This is due largely to the efforts of one man,
Yves Coutarel, who is cultural representative
both for the town and for the Association Nationale pour la Preservation des Monuments et
Sites Historiques. Responsible for the cultural
manifestations of the city, he defines "culture"
as open-mindedness and a curiosity about the

All around Saint-Paul-de-Mausole,
the municipality of Saint-Rémy has posted reproductions of Van Gogh's canvases
at the spot where they were painted.
A view of the monastery was painted from here.

world in its many aspects, including gardens. The result has been seven straight years of first prizes in the departmental competitions for towns of ten to thirty thousand people. The municipal greenhouses and a team of five gardeners produce many of the plants from seed that deck traffic islands, the inner courtyards of apartment complexes, public buildings and of course the public parks and gardens of the city. Begonias, ageratum and scarlet sage have been banished, replaced by fragrant pastel petunias (lining the windows of the Renaissance town hall) or nicotianas, decorative tobacco plants, eight hundred at a time, intoxicating passersby on summer evenings. Intersections at the approaches to town have round rose beds of different colors (Milrose, Iceberg, Bernadette Chirac) underplanted with perennials such as deep-blue leadwort. A classic city square with benches and shade trees is decked with original floral borders mixing cleomes, *Sola-*

num rantonnettii with its non-stop mauve-blue potato flowers, white and purple spring violets, scented white tobacco plants, all in subtle blendings of hues.

In the old cloister of the Cordeliers, regularly changing art exhibits give onto a central courtyard featuring climbing New Dawns on all the pillars, meeting deeper pink geraniums on the window ledges above. This cloister has been cut in half, and a blind wall faces the gallery windows. Undaunted by this abrupt separation, Coutarel has used it as the backdrop for a sophisticated display of foliage and subtle color around basins: fuchsias, more solanum, dimorphothecas and strong foliage plants like dwarf fan palms.

Tarascon has become celebrated also for its annual flower fair, held every Whitsun weekend since 1983. Nurseries, horticultural specialists, artisans whose creations use fresh flowers (in soaps, perfumes, dried bouquets, honey, candles, et cetera) gather on the boulevards surrounding the city center. From seventeen stands the first year to one hundred and twenty in 1989, this fair has met with tremendous success. Now three bulb specialists come all the way from Holland, and there is more and more originality in the plants proposed—one man, for example, brings eight or ten varieties of nothing but cuphea!

One focus for all this activity is Tarascon's major monument, the fifteenth-century castle of Good King René. This "bon vivant" transformed his medieval keep into yet another pleasure palace, where the massive stone fireplaces had a special

*The municipality of Tarascon
has installed an art gallery in the old cloister of the Cordeliers. New Dawn
roses climb the pillars, meeting
deep-pink geraniums on the window ledges above (top).
The annual flower fair in Tarascon
draws ever-increasing numbers of plant specialists from all over Europe, and local
connoisseurs often find treasures here (above).*

niche in the wall for the heating of mulled wine. The courtyard garden was composed of formal squares planted with decorative, medicinal and aromatic essences around a basin and a fountain. At the far end stood a large bird cage. Yves Coutarel is advising on the restoration of this garden, complete with the ornamental white peacocks so sought after by the monarch. (The king also had ostriches, but the spirit of historical authenticity can only go so far.)

Tarascon's example is an inspiration to other municipalities with their heavily watered lawns, and its fair has greatly enriched private gardens all over the region. Probably the least well-known of these are the ones that grow unsuspected in the very heart of Provençal towns and cities.

PRIVATE SHOW

From the gardens of the Rochers des Doms in Avignon, anyone looking down on the city roofs discovers an astonishing number of tall shade trees, surrounded by spreading greenery. In *Les Amants d'Avignon* Elsa Triolet described her lovers wandering "among these narrow streets twisted like arms, between walls where France, Italy and Spain mingled and protected each other, stone wearing its glory and its downfall in Gothic menace, the sensual folly of the baroque, sometimes grimacing in a gargoyle,

The orangery of a seventeenth-century townhouse garden in Avignon has become a separate residence today. Tall shade trees filter dappled light on a nineteenth-century basin (top). Many old townhouses have retained fine architectural detailing such as these elegant steps, which lead to a small but sophisticated shade garden (above).

sometimes modeled like bread dough. Stone ramparts, churches, secretive old townhouses, interior courtyards, gardens behind high walls, extending a green branch here and there. . . . "

All these cities contain private gardens—often quite large, though all but invisible from the street. High "honey-colored, rose-faded walls" protect them, whose crumbling plaster supports cascading ivies, wisterias and Virginia creepers. The public passages that border them have their own charm, of course; Avignon's Rue Saluce in the heart of town is like a winding country lane. But even off busier thoroughfares, southern cities contrast the glare and bustle of the street with private mysteries of verdant shade. Sometimes an elegant door is enough to suggest a world beyond. . . .

Provençal cities possess seventeenth and eighteenth-century townhouses in rich quantity. Their models have been sometimes French and sometimes Italian, with many variations on both. The Musée Calvet in Avignon has kept its

French design: a public entrance courtyard behind a majestic gate encircled by stables and servants' quarters, with the private garden hidden on the other side of the main building. The romantic plantings that Stendhal admired there have been changed several times since, and are now undergoing transformation once again. Other residences, following Italian inspiration, have a secret courtyard enclosed within four walls, like the eighteenth-century courtyard of the elegant Hôtel d'Europe, in which a wisteria-draped fountain murmurs for diners shaded by the massive canopy of a beautifully pruned plane tree. Both types of townhouse may use pavings made of Rhône pebbles, or *calades*, often arranged into decorative motifs (one pictures Halley's comet). Whether these inviting spaces can be called gardens depends on how much stone you will allow in proportion to vegetation.

The larger townhouses had greenery to spare. Some have since been subdivided, but a

*The private garden of the former cloister
of Notre Dame next to the Pope's Palace in Avignon has pleasant nooks sheltered
by the medieval apse, and, in the distance, a Roman well.*

surprising number still exist in their entirety, often with an elegant fountain or nymphaea at the far end to provide a focus from the house windows. The seventeenth and eighteenth-century façades that face the garden are among any city's finest, and the nymphaeas are a delight. What originally lay between is difficult to guess—little evidence remains. What can a modern gardener hope to accomplish in such a setting? These owners are rarely the kind of people who buy up farmsteads and village houses. Often descendants of old local families, they belong to that still vital old Provence that many new settlers never encounter. Many have kept their *campagnes* or country estates, which remain as discreet as their city residences. Other townhouses belong in surprising proportion to antique dealers, or recently transferred representatives of government services or national networks such as banks that put them in close contact with the local establishment. Some have become semi-public, like the old convent garden transformed into the CELA language institute in Avignon, whose shaded park (vast for the center city) contains an amusing example of Belle Epoque *rocaille*, or cement rockery.

Plantings in these gardens still make much of Anduze pottery, which now fetches unbelievable prices. They combine formal layout with the modern taste for steady color, usually oleanders and geraniums. Many are now enjoyed in summer, and their owners welcome shade—luckily, for a good number lie nestled between the high walls of subdivided courtyards, or under the spreading shade of centuries-old deciduous trees.

In many of these gardens there is a sense of fragmented and layered time. Fragments and layers are exactly what one ambitious Avignon gardener found in an old townhouse courtyard when he sought to uncover the base of an eighteenth-century niche. The Comte de Brion began this project at the age of 68, digging up

The courtyard of the elegant Hôtel d'Europe in Avignon, framed by a spectacular plane tree, serves as a dining terrace in summer, when it is a favorite rendez-vous for festival-goers.

some two hundred square meters of soil, carrying it off to his country property in an old Peugeot. . . . And thus he happened on curious fragments of blue and white ceramic. When the archaeologists took over the site, they found distinct levels of deposits from prehistoric times to the nineteenth century—glass, earthenware, human bones, notably an exceptional collection of quite beautiful medieval pottery. Some twenty years later, the count allowed these findings to go on show, and began to put his garden back together. He now understands why his mother, as he recalls, was constantly frustrated at not being able to root trees in this courtyard. . . . The conditions of townhouse gardening can be quite particular.

Many old city gardens incorporate the past more conveniently, having been designed around sections of famous monuments. The gardens of the former cloister of Notre Dame des Doms in Avignon, close to the public park but not open to visits, spread their formal parterres

around the church's apse, with crenellated walls of the Pope's Palace as a backdrop. The old cloister once stood on this spot, around a 35-meter-deep Roman well that was once part of a pagan temple to Hercules. The apse frames a statue of the Virgin, girded in front by two formal horseshoes of low box hedging. Dwarf box also encloses beds of roses, oleanders, petunias, four o'clocks, bergenias. Height is provided by pencil cypresses that must be bought each year for the Christmas crèche in the church and would thereafter remain homeless, if not planted out in the garden—a southern version of the eternal northern Christmas tree problem! At the far end of the garden, a group of olive trees is bordered with euryops (yellow daisy flowers) and backed by a row of newly planted pomegranates. There is an intimate, shaded patio with a variety of fuchsias in pots, a small greenhouse. A sheltered corner of the house is swathed in sky-blue *Plumbago capensis*, behind a huge knot of pink oleanders.

In the Pochy's unusual cloister garden in Avignon,
nineteenth-century palms have become the focal point for a clever design that makes
the space seem much larger than it is (above).
In Nîmes, a nineteenth-century exotic winter garden is built into an older
townhouse, so that it remains half indoors, half out.
The plantings can be viewed from an ornate balcony (following page).

Wind can be a problem in this rather exposed, hilltop garden, in spite of its high walls
on three sides. From the fourth, one can easily
see as far as Mont Ventoux. From the house entrance, which gives in fact onto the lowest level
of the public Jardin des Doms, one can have no
idea that such a large and varied garden lies
behind. A peahen, however, once made the discovery, flying over the wall and settling herself
comfortably into the household, preferring its
privacy to the park from which she came. From
the Rue Banasterie far below, the Christmas
cypresses stand out strikingly against the apse
in a halo of dark blue sky—a popular photograph
for passing tourists.

Very different treatment has been given to
an old cloister, later incorporated into a neoclassical townhouse. Decorators Marian and
Yves Pochy have made it into an exotic garden.
Here the ancient arches, now painted in elegant, pastel salmon and blue with green shutters, give onto a central space grouped around
five large palm trees, survivors from an earlier
period. This focal point is on a slightly lower
level from the broad house terrace used for
dining. The family can also view the garden
from an upper gallery on three sides, the fourth
being closed off by a blind wall that shows only
the tops of the neighbors' trees. Lindens and
junipers add mass and shade in the center, where
irregular island plantings surround the palms
with oleanders, pittosporums and arbutus mingled with jasmine, Fairy roses, bergenia, blue-
bells and columbines. *Trachelospermum jasminoides* provides fragrant ground cover. The
diagonals used in this design along with the exuberance of the plantings make the space seem much
larger than it is.

The surrounding walls are also densely planted, with shade-lovers like acanthus and perennial geraniums at their feet. Under the arches,
they have been paved with special *tedlakt* tiles
from Marrakesh. One of the garden's successes
is the Moorish basin that lies under the shade of
the cloister roof, but extends one broad tongue
around one column into the garden outside.
This serves as an elegant swimming pool. Nor is
this the most surprising effect: Mme. Pochy has

added some unusual, witty *trompe-l'oeil* decoration, in particular a fine figure of Woody Allen
looking down, keeping anxious watch on swimmers and strollers below and on the other spec-
tators seated on the raised patio. His presence
certainly adds to this garden's theatricality.

Another exotic garden has been installed in
Nîmes in a townhouse under a glass roof, an elegant "winter garden," nurtured by generations
of an ancient family. From its walls hang layer
upon layer of strongly designed cooling foliage.
A veritable grotto is planted with a fruit-produc-
ing phellodendron. There are various rubber
plants, avocadoes and banana trees, and *Celi-
ganella mexicana* (licopode). The show can be
viewed from a raised, formal patio whose
columns and antique patio furniture mark the
transition between indoor and half-outdoor
spaces.

Restored townhouse gardens in Provence
have kept a certain unity of style in their rec-

*In southern cities one often sees
"suspended" or second-story gardens, visible as patches of greenery above the street.
The eighteenth-century prefecture
buildings in Avignon house a lovely one, viewed here from within.*

tangular shape behind high walls, their double viewpoint (from ground level and from the first story overlooking the garden), their strong mineral element in fountains, wells and earthenware pots, and the impression they often give of moist and murky depths: these are shade gardens, with water at their feet, far removed from any popular southern stereotype. The larger ones include small replicas of château parks with their layered greenery, pines, oaks and box. Foliage and stone, with all their soft nuances of beige, gray, green, cream and gold, create the peculiar atmosphere that is both formal and intimate, secretive and dramatic. Only rarely is there strong color and this, in the form of oleanders and geraniums, is generally a recent addition. Only a few of these gardens have inspired original modern plantings, and a great many remain rather neglected, their clumps of old shrubs mingling with impressive stone masses for majestic effect nonetheless.

City gardeners today are not limiting themselves to the restoration of old townhouses, however. Some have bought several simpler houses, as is common in villages, keeping the ruins of one or more as the foundation of a courtyard that is not as formal as those of the old aristocracy, nor as rustic as village ones. Like the latter, its spaces are more haphazard and irregular than those planned by neoclassical architects. Town gardens generally have a different scale from their country cousins, however, with more space on the ground, even if wall plantings are crucial. There may be an elegant terrace with steps leading down into the main garden, a large central basin—elements that suggest greater formality than in the usual village plot, which must generally cope with steeper terrain.

Yves Coutarel in Tarascon has transformed a group of old houses into an original private garden, with the help of his friend the painter Bob Parkinson, who does most of the actual spadework. This is first of all a vertical garden, however, and one in which fragrance and sound (water trickling in the large central basin, with its arums and water lilies) have not been forgotten. Old roses (Belle de Londres, Wedding Day), wisteria, a variety of honeysuckles and jasmines climb up the pale stone. Colors are almost always pastel or white, which makes this a lovely garden for summer evenings. Many exotics thrive here in small spaces, planted around the stepping-stones that cross the small lawn. The high walls give a sense of enclosure and division yet there is openness, nothing oppressive. The view from the three-story house embraces the entire garden and the roofs beyond, but the view of the house from the garden, with its Mermaid rose and *Hydrangea petiolaris*, is equally important. No one angle of vision dominates.

A third major vantage point has just been added. Until recently, the far wall was covered by a magnificent Bobby James rose, brought from England years ago. The ruin beyond this wall has since been purchased, and has been transformed into an upper platform, opposite the second-story house windows. The Bobby

Lawrence Durrell enjoyed
"summer-houses completely brambled-in by roses and honeysuckle, statues covered
in green ivy with only one free ankle left to
view . . . where the coming and going of the birds made one feel one was
in the heart of virgin jungle."
Such gardens exist in the heart of all Provençal cities.

James is being retrained around this new space.

The ground level has the most complex plantings, with the palette familiar by now from Coutarel's other works: pale blue plumbagos, deeper ceanothus, Marguerite Hilling, Nevada and Iceberg roses, and of course white and green trumpets of nicotianas. Variegated ivy and periwinkles provide winter color.

In Lambesc, the sedate and elegant façade of a solid bourgeois house protected by the city's ramparts hides a sophisticated garden created by Robert Reyre. High walls, of course, support ivies and old climbing roses (including the frequent single-flowered one that resembles American Pillar); but there is also a double-flowered variegated pomegranate trained almost as a climber. In the walls themselves, deep niches shelter statues—for this is also a sculpture garden. Above all, however, its character comes from the planters and pots that brim with magnificent datura trumpets, cascading fuch-

sias and mounded chrysanthemums, artistically arranged around the elegant furniture. The plants all have structural character, but are planned mostly for summer brilliance. In the fall, the deep wine hue of Virginia creepers provides another dramatic, contrasting setting for this garden.

Some town courtyards have kept something of a cottage garden atmosphere in their rich and tumbling, multicolored and, in the Provençal variant, many-leveled array of plants. One such astonishing tiny garden is reached by a long narrow passage emerging suddenly onto a well of sun and dappled shade. The central basin is surrounded by impatiens; a trellised rose forms a ceiling overhead, and there are hanging pots of fuchsias and geraniums. Still farther above is the house balcony crowded with more geraniums, fuchsias, and plumbagos creeping up the wall. The plantings themselves form a spiral around the central basin. This miniature garden is surprisingly dense, bright and unexpected.

Villeneuve-les-Avignon (half town, half village) has many appealing small courtyards off its main street, parts of old cardinals' residences and convents with wells and chapels. Other small towns like Le Paradou also hide such rich inner courtyards, one of which is sheltered enough for bougainvillea and a much-beloved collection of perennials mixed with rare irises. Or nearby, a long, narrow courtyard garden features the peeling trunks of late-flowering lagerstoemia that provide linear rhythms for climbing roses, pittosporum, mixed bulbs and perennials.

Provençal cities, like those all over France, have their outlying bands of suburban villas with their inevitable weeping willows and forsythias. But one modern house, not far from Van Gogh's monastery outside Saint-Rémy, has been surrounded by a varied garden designed by a local doctor's wife, Madame Fillipini. Packed into a series of tiny spaces, it provides each with its own character and seasonal emphasis, for the pleasures of eating outdoors, swimming, gazing at the view of orchards and the Alpilles beyond floral display (many types of sage grouped in

Water trickles into a large central basin
planted with arums and water lilies in a walled garden in Tarascon.
Old roses (Belle de Londres, Wedding Day), wisteria,
a variety of honeysuckles and jasmines climb the pale stone
of this Tarascon town garden.

front of a blue cypress cone). One of its best features is its tapestry hedge, finest in the autumn with the berries of cotoneaster and *Arbutus unedo*, the tonal mixtures of box and elaeagnus. But climbing roses (Pompon de Paris) and honeysuckle extend its delights into other seasons. The rural outskirts of Saint-Rémy contain many more sophisticated properties belonging to some of the most famous gardeners and designers of the western world, but this one is the result of one individual's personal efforts, with limited space and budget, to create detail by detail, season by season, a densely textured and varied garden fabric.

Other cities could have been selected here, both for their private and public plantings, including Orange, Bagnols, Vaison, Carpentras, and Cavaillon, each with its particular character and site. The gardens of Aix and Marseille have already received considerable attention elsewhere. Indeed, the variety of Provençal city gardens is inexhaustible—they include the most

conservative, perhaps the most neglected, sometimes the most spectacular and also the most discreet. Their spaces are subject to definite constraints and present special challenges. But their show is becoming richer and richer, as more city gardeners are becoming connoisseurs and collectors, eager to display their treasures in these unusual settings.

*In a courtyard near Aix,
deep niches shelter statues—for, among the profusion of pots and urns,
this is also a sculpture garden (top).
Creeping verbena provides one of the most reliable pot
plants for the region (above).*

*A suburban gardener near Saint-Rémy has made
artful use of small spaces for family enjoyment as well as lush garden texture.*

PARADISE
TODAY

Provence has been a crossroads from its earliest human habitation. Ligurians, Greeks, Celts, Romans, Franks—all came, stayed, added something to the melting pot; later it was Italians, Armenians, consumptive English and Russians. . . . Colette put it very well: "What a country!" she wrote in the 1920s. "The invader endows it with villas and garages, with motorcars and dance-halls built to look like *mas*. The barbarians from the north parcel out the land, speculate and deforest, and that is certainly a great pity. But during the course of the centuries how many ravishers have not fallen in love with such a captive? They arrive plotting to ruin her, stop suddenly and listen to her breathing in her sleep, and then, turning silent and respectful, they softly shut the gate in the fence. Submissive to your wishes, Provence, they fasten on your vine-leaf crown again, replant the pine tree and the fig, sow the variegated melon and have no

other desire, Beauty, than to serve you and enjoy it."

The garden traditions of Provence bear witness to the region's amazing capacity for both permanence and change. Today, the area is still drawing new residents from all over the globe who will also be absorbed, for further enrichment. Those with sufficient resources and leisure inevitably create a garden, in accordance with a vogue that now holds sway in most of the western world. But if newcomers have introduced this fashion to Provence, natives have also adopted it with enthusiasm: thus old local families, with their roots deep in the soil, redesign a corner of the old château garden around a new swimming pool. . . .

The "elements" continue to determine choices—how could it be otherwise? The rigors of the weather take many new gardeners by surprise. The cold snap of the mid-1980s did away with many fine collections of ceanothus and shrubby veronicas, even affecting some ancient olive trees. The drought years that followed have increased the concern for both quality and quantity of water (the demand for drinking water alone increases ten times in the summer months here). Climate and soil impose constraints on the most adventuresome.

In this part of the south, few expatriate gardeners have indulged in the sometimes surrealistic fantasies that proliferated on the Côte d'Azur in the 1920s and the 1930s. In most cases, pre-existing buildings are restored, the garden is planned around a former farm, often, as already seen, preserving vines, orchards, lavender fields. Local stone and old tiles are preferred to uniform, mass-produced building materials, though garden sculpture, a natural addition for those who love the mineral element, may come from the four corners of the earth and from every epoch. Many of these gardens are resolutely cosmopolitan, and belong to people who also own properties in other parts of the globe. And yet the general tendency seems to be harmony with the rural landscape, which was often a major reason for choosing the site in the first place. With some exceptions, these gardens remain concentrations of the surrounding

Ipomoea, cosmos and solidago—these
three stalwarts of summer gardens are here set against Provençal clay and tiles
in the garden of Mr. C (above).
Delicate colors abound in the garden of landscape
architect Michel Semini (opposite).

countryside rather than an effort to rise above and exclude it. The old dream of flower and fruit continues to determine the general mood of the neo-Provençal garden, but recent creations are more decidedly decorative, more self-consciously sophisticated and, above all, more deliberately varied in their textures.

LOCAL COLOR

The greatest break with the past in southern gardens today must be the emphasis on summer and its cult of the sun. Many property owners come mainly for the hot months, and require, as a result, abundant and constant bloom in what was once a near-dormant period. The Riviera already experienced this shift of interest in the 1920s, when summer tourism began to replace the winter season. But the Côte d'Azur has a subtropical climate in which brilliant, heat-loving treasures can expect to survive the winter; the inland areas are merely Mediterranean.

The natural cycle of the vegetation cannot change to suit fashion, and continues to produce its best bloom in spring and fall. No matter what efforts are extended, floral display in Provence will always be at its height at those times—at least at its freshest, since mid-summer temperatures often stop all growth, even where water is plentiful. Of course, many southern gardeners still consider May and June their finest months.

Summer sun worshipers generally concentrate their efforts on two main sections: the patio by the house and the swimming pool area. The former perpetrates the old usage of earthenware pots, now even more plentiful, less formally arranged, and containing a much wider variety of plants. As for swimming pools, they now form an integral part of southern garden design, a focus for floral display. They long ago lost their connotations of Hollywoodian splashiness and nouveau-riche vulgarity, and can be afforded by a wide range of people. All but the oldest residents have succumbed to the

Summer color is reflected on terracotta pots and vases of soft glazes and rich volumes at the Antonin nursery. On the terrace that typically completes the façade of a Provençal dwelling, however humble or grand, pot gardening means easy, though frequent, watering.

appeal of the midday swim, without which August in Provence means hiding behind closed shutters as if besieged.

Far from being showy, Provençal pools are generally hidden from the house. Terracing provides the answer in many cases, as both can be located on a different level. In the garden of English designer Sir Terence Conran, the steps leading up to the pool are monumental and processional, graced by terracotta urns from Athens, the dimensions of which completely dwarf the local production. Canals on either side allow water to cascade to an ornamental basin below, emphasizing this main axis in the design. In couturier Bernard Perris's garden near Saint-Rémy, digging conditions made it necessary to build the pool on a high platform that is now clothed in Virginia creeper and surrounded with roses. A dovecote and dramatic statuary frame one side, while on the other a pergola shades the bathhouse, scenting it with roses, jasmine, and wisteria. The water remains

invisible from any distance, but swimmers can see formal lavender beds laid out at their feet. On the other hand, the platform setting means wind exposure, and the mistral can play havoc with the garden furniture.

Near Mouriès, the owner of an elegant old *mas* has half buried her pool to hide it both from the house and the wind. It is reached by descending a few steps under an arch of

*Swimming pools offer an ideal synthesis
between indoor and outdoor summer life, activity and rest, allowing even the heat
of the day to add pleasure to these gardens
that cater to all the senses, as here at designer Terence Conran's mas (top).
A seventeenth-century pool house at the
Petit Fontanille provides a particularly fine focal point, visible from many parts
of the garden, though the pool itself is not (above).*

cotoneaster and banksia roses. The slopes surrounding the water on two sides are planted with cistus, coreopsis, lavender and other colorful low shrubs and perennials. A single ancient olive at the far end shades the path that leads to the tennis courts, and the sunken bathhouse, over which tumbles fragrant jasmine, completes the frame.

In other properties, the path leads downhill. At the elaborate Val Joanis garden in the Luberon, it meanders along four different terraces before reaching the well of sun and filtered shade that surrounds the pool.

Other designers hide the pool entirely behind high walls for maximum discretion and shelter. This is a natural solution for those whose properties have retained the cypress compartments of market gardens, or old, walled vegetable gardens.

Château properties often have enclosed vegetable plots that can be thus transformed. A more ordinary solution where the topography allows it is to put the pool around a corner, still against a south-facing wall, still accessible through the garden. Thus it has easy access without stairs, but is still out of sight and hearing. Sometimes, however, it is directly in front of the house, hidden in the garden design much like Edgar Allen Poe's stolen letter. Thus a modern, Palladian-inspired horseshoe-shaped house stands directly opposite the sudden and striking rise of the Alpilles, with the pool between the two. Its inside is painted . . . black. Surprisingly, this is most effective, creating a shadowy but not somber impression that makes the water seem a natural garden feature, not a recreational adjunct. Other owners, such as designer Dick Dumas, have preferred navy blue liners for similar effect.

Thus the ancient water gods are served today by new rituals of immersion. Of course swimming pools, like vast expanses of lawn, can be an ostentatious display of wealth in an area where water is scarce—and certainly water has

Swimming pools are invariably hidden from the house in a variety of ways, forming a secluded and separate oasis, as here in the garden of Jacques Grange.

at times been a source of dispute between vacationers and farmers. Owners often dig new wells—as deep as 150 meters—to find what they need for both pool, lawn and long-flowering mixed borders. These gardeners are perhaps pushing nature to new extremes, and nature may collaborate more or less willingly. But Mediterranean gardens have often been oases of refreshment, and today's pools in a sense continue this tradition.

The strategies for achieving an abundance of summer color, whether for patio or pool, are numerous. Many gardeners acclimatize subtropical plants—pelargoniums and oleanders have provided the most common solution for many generations. These may be taken indoors, planted in particularly sheltered places, or replaced when a cold snap in winter does them in. Other plants of borderline hardiness, borrowed not only from the Riviera but from California, New Zealand, South Africa and Chile, have become common in summer gardens: hibiscus, blue agathaea (felicia), dimorphotheca, gazania, delosperma, phygelius, the late-flowering ceanothus and crape myrtles (both called summer lilacs, the latter often used in town plantings). Less often, bougainvilleas, tibouchinas, callistemons and cuphea add dazzling hues. Then again, many plants that flower in late summer or fall elsewhere begin in July in Provence: blue plumbagos and leadworts, for example, agapanthus and many of the late-blooming sages. And some perennials that are stalwarts elsewhere flourish here as well: nepetas, *Centranthus ruber*, Japanese anemones, achillea and day lilies. There

are also summer-flowering trees: catalpas, sophoras, acacias, koelreuteria, and inevitably, the blessing of lavenders in their many varieties, with their reassuring echoes of rural roots and their brilliance in early summer.

The color question has taken on tremendous importance in southern gardening today. Two definite "schools" dominate new creations (though many successful gardens remain independent of both). The first espouses strong, cheerful hues: orange, red, yellow, turquoise, hard blues and bright greens, which now suggest Mediterranean sunshine to lovers of Provence in many far-off countries. Fashionable Provençal fabrics, based on eighteenth-century designs and traditions, have today established an international reputation for their gorgeous array of colors, although originally their dominants were navies, browns and blacks. Of the two main companies that manufacture them, Olivades has kept to the more traditional, subdued range

The strong contrasts and bright hues of Van Gogh's work, including his famous sunflowers, have inspired an entire school of Provençal gardeners (top). One of the region's finest eighteenth-century domains near Saint-Rémy includes a modern summer garden around the pool. It is reached by a path lined with slim cypresses and lavender flowers and edged with ancient fruit trees (above).

while the Demery family, creators for generations of the Souleiado line (commercialized in America as Pierre Deux), appeal by their rich reds, greens, blues, oranges, yellows. The Demerys have long had connections with the Alpilles town of Le Paradou, where buildings are often tinted with vivid local pigments. All over the area, in fact, where natural ocher beds can be found, whole villages may sport these colors—Roussillon is the most famous example. Houses remodeled today that follow this trend favor intense orange washes with bright blue shutters, and a riot of flower color.

This "school" can be linked to the popular image of Van Gogh, who came seeking in the southern light the clear hues of Japanese prints. For the painter, these remained strong even in the drought of high summer. And we have seen that Arles provided him with a good range of gay summer bloom, perhaps because he was drawn to peasant gardens, where even today pelargoniums are at their most dazzling. The difference today, perhaps, for wealthier and more ambitious gardeners, is their quest for brightness in continuous abundance, and not only in small spaces as seasonal accents.

The house and garden of Sir Terence Conran, designer, founder of Habitat, writer and well-known francophile, illustrates this approach to Provençal color. Not surprisingly, the Demerys helped him find the property. The spreading *mas* near Le Paradou, first viewed along a lane of magnificent horse chestnuts, has adapted the fiery orange and bright blue shutters of this school. Existing pigeon holes under the eaves have been clearly outlined in white, others painted on to match. On the south side lies a small plot of flowers left by the original peasant owner. Conran's landscaping has been concentrated to the north, where a slope rises rather abruptly to the Canal du Midi at its crest. This provides ample water for the aforementioned swimming pool, with its esplanade of broad steps. The excellent proportions of this

Designer Terence Conran's garden
in Maussane provides brilliant color all season long with banks of iris,
cascades of wisteria, albizzia vaults,
red roses, phlomis, Russian sage and many-hued oleander.

sequence of constructions bears witness to Conran's talents as a landscape designer, though the monumental mood is untypical of Provençal gardens. More intimate spaces will gradually mature alongside, such as sunken rectangles edged with running water under canopies of spreading planes. Here Mr. Conran explains that it will be pleasant "to sit and read, eat lunch in the shade, draw, paint, write, and amuse the children with games."

Along the path to the west, an easy-care mixture for summer display blends pink lavateras, bright blue perovksia, cistus, pink jasmine, thymes and sages, verbenas, both green and silver santolinas mingling with the silver fountains of cardoons. Catnip mingles with cerise roses and more irises. An olive orchard occupies a square in front of the house, happily underplanted with pink-flowered cistus, teucrium, hibiscus, perovskia again, with contrasting groups of red-leaved *Rosa rubrifolia*.

Annuals may play an important role in cre-

ating a profusion of bright color, not only pelargoniums but lantana, verbenas, petunias, sages, cosmos, nigella. One of the brightest, most cheerful gardens in Provence is a riot of color from spring to fall, planted by the wife of painter Joseph Bayol for the pleasure and inspiration of her husband. It consists of a large front yard (about 1,000 square meters), traversed by a small stream, with a willow, cherry trees, a

*In the Conran garden, canals line
the monumental steps linking the house below and the pool hidden above,
an original feature of this garden's strong design (above).
The Conran mas has been restored with the orange and blue hues
now in fashion (above and opposite).
Painter Joseph Bayol finds rich inspiration in the colorful garden planted
by his wife for his enjoyment (following page).*

yellows, and one, indicating a bright patch, explains apologetically: "My husband likes red flowers. . . ."

Owners of the pale persuasion still want continual summer bloom. One cherishes a particularly subtle, cream-colored variety of oleander. Even annual flowers, so often developed precisely for their prolonged display of high color, are now selected for pastels. At the Petit Fontanille garden near Tarascon, a special dwarf cosmos has been developed that bears the name of the property. Here nurseryman Ryan Gainey has helped the owner, Ann Cox Chambers, select annuals and biennials for their everpaler tones. He named the "Immerson White" foxglove (a cross between *Digitalis purpurea alba* and *D. mertonensis*) for the street he lives on in Atlanta, Georgia. Mr. Gainey agrees in theory that bright color is appropriate for the southern sun, and admires fields of rape and poppies among olives and cypresses in spring;

pink-flowering horse chestnut and three redbuds. In this setting thrives an abundance of annual and perennial flowers, in a lovely alternance of deep shade and bright sun. Columbines and delphiniums, ornamental garlic, poppies—and cherries, in blossom and in fruit—give way to cosmos, impatiens, sages, zinnias, day lilies, achillea, Japanese anemones. The pond sustains papyrus, water lilies, *Iris pseudacorus* collected in the wild. Even at the end of winter, the space is full of bulbs, and, needless to say, all wildflowers are welcome. Small footpaths meander through this garden, giving views onto the house with its trellis, patio and teal-blue shutters. This space is joyous, exuberant, and stimulating—a kind of cross between an English cottage garden and a Provençal *mas*.

Color and light are of course inseparable in any garden. The "Van Gogh" trend, with its tendency toward sun worship, seems to introduce the power and warmth of Provençal sunshine into the most shaded corners, as if the sun's magic intensity were somehow embodied in brilliant bloom. Are today's vivid Provençal gardens a more sophisticated version of the peasant taste Van Gogh knew and loved, or the elaboration of a gay, modern, holiday image imported into Provence? Perhaps both, at the same time.

Directly opposed to this is the school that admires only the palest pastels and whites in settings of evergreen and evergray foliage. Here too fashion plays a part: numerous garden owners sniff at the idea of oranges and strong

The intimate patio of decorator Raffi is a delightful blend of colorful perennials and small shrubs overflowing pots and stone troughs, contrasting elegantly with the deliberately faded gray-blue paint of the deck furniture (top).

but in this richly textured garden where he now advises, reds and oranges occur only as foliage tones or in outlying areas (roses in the cutting garden, nasturtiums in the apricot orchard).

The school of muted color also plans its effects for other seasons, even winter. Stone and foliage count at least as much as blossom, both for luminosity and texture. Moreover, while it may be said that the Van Gogh tendency derives in part from traditional farm gardens, this opposing trend owes much of its inspiration to the wild landscapes of the Mediterranean, as if the garden were now a concentration of the *garrigue* instead of the farmyard. At the same time, these paler gardens invariably contain formal elements, the kind of plant sculpture to which *garrigue* plants lend themselves so beautifully. In this they are perhaps inspired as well by the refinement of traditional château gardens, which usually do not feature brilliant floral display. The Provençal light they value is not dazzling but, in the happy phrase of one gardener, "Virgilian." Their search for strong forms combined with ever-finer color nuances, and their love of gray, recall Cézanne rather than Van Gogh.

Roderick Cameron and Gabriel Occelli created the model for this school in their famous Luberon garden the Quatre Sources, which began as an oak forest on a wild, terraced hillside. Already at La Fiorentina and Clos Fiorentina on Cap Ferrat, gardens Cameron designed before he left for Provence, green and white were chosen as the dominant tones, complemented by various blues, silvers and pale pink. In the Luberon property, retaining walls and connecting staircases were repaired and built, and trees were thinned to allow views of the surrounding countryside and the dramatic hilltown across the valley. Thousands of bulbs were planted—dwarf tulips, crocus, iris.

The path zigzags down the hill, under the shade of the oaks that predominate in the wood (with pines on the lower levels), along drystone terraces rich with cistus, myrtles, box,

The patio garden of furniture designer Dick Dumas
in Oppède, with a dramatic view of the medieval ruined village rising above.
White impatiens in shade, pale pelargoniums in sun
provide summer flowering. Even the mulberries and cypresses have had
their trunks whitewashed (above and opposite, bottom).

rosemary—all the local wild vegetation. But each species constitutes an entire collection—*Cistus monspeliensis*, *C. aguilari*, *C. albidus* and the uncommon *C. palhinhae*, among others. All of this has been enriched by an amazing quantity of rare plants that blend happily with the atmosphere of natural woodland. Structure in this plenitude is provided by stone contours: the walls themselves and the vaulting of two springs, much like those of the bories in the surrounding hills, and above all by the strong, irregular lines of the tree trunks rising from the low, descending, horizontal lines of the terraces.

Interestingly, this wild profusion has a number of formal elements for contrast. There are boxwood balls and yew cones on the raised walls, and a formal rectangle of alternating green and silver santolinas below the main downward path. The angles of the house contain no less than three courtyard gardens.

This extremely refined garden underwent a period of abandonment before becoming the

property of Mr. and Mrs. Nicolas Krul. It had become overgrown with brambles, and three truckloads of dead shrubs had to be removed. The lowest terraces have not yet been recuperated. An orchard has been planted on the other side of the house from the main hillside garden, which will have iris and oleander borders. Clusters of white roses have been added. Much of the woodland has been pruned to let in more

The famous Quatre Sources garden
on a terraced hillside in the Luberon is rich with unusual berberis, mahonias,
sages, brooms, prunus, contoneasters, roses, loniceras,
euphorbias, junipers, variegated myrtles and hollies, phlomis,
and photinias, to name but a few (top).

light and show off the beauty of the trees. This was a garden whose character had become almost legendary in the region. The Kruls are making peace with ghosts, protecting the collections, but inevitably imposing their own enthusiasms—and colors. It will remain one of the most original gardens of Provence.

An extraordinary garden and a wonderful example of the muted color school has been created not far away by Madame de Vésian, a talented woman who combines fancy and form in a delightfully personal manner. In the intimate spaces surrounding a typical village house—a narrow passage south, and small terraces extending on either side—she has turned the common *garrigue* aromatics, evergreens and evergrays, into a series of sculptures that comprises a carefully designed ensemble. Here formal pruning is simply the gentle directive of an imagination full of liveliness and verve, a guide that never imposes constraints. The plants are obviously content and thriving—domes of iberis, german-

ders, santolinas, and catnips mingle with iris, *Lonicera pileata* and laurel around an old well. On the summit of a low outer wall, *Convolvulus cneorum*, cineraria, rosemaries and lavenders (only the white ones here), spread luxuriantly. Trees are handled in the same manner: a tall local juniper is shaped like a huge gumdrop, a smaller one like a lollipop, while an old *Arbutus unedo* has its several, reddish, gnarled trunks exposed in its open center. Slim tunnels of cypress add vertical emphasis—all in contrast to the wild pines and oaks across the narrow valley, though in the midst of the distant scrubland, like a discreet echo, stand two similar cypress columns.

The surrounding *garrigue* provides a model in the rounded slopes of its hills and its subtle grays, beiges and dark greens, colors that are mirrored and accentuated around the house. Madame de Vésian allows some touches of bright color in season, like a *Feijoa sellowiana*, a lush red ball beside a path, or one brilliant

*The Quatre Sources garden
features ivies and vines, stands of fleshy Sedum spectabile, blankets of
creeping thymes, pink and yellow-flowering
lamiums, and hellebores. The "shelves" created by retaining walls, raised
for easy viewing, display minuscule treasures.*

Near Bonnieux, Nicole de Vésian
has created an amazing blend of stone, foliage and flower that echoes the tones
and forms of the surrounding landscape.
This garden possesses a very sophisticated garden texture.

luminous tone sets off the foliage to perfection. Everywhere are rounded forms: white stone balls dot the garden at various levels. This garden is like those of medieval cloisters: in its magical spaces, earth meets sky, wilderness is lovingly tamed into art, and all the elements, earth, stone and vegetation, live together in peaceful reciprocity. Personal inspiration and local tradition have met harmoniously, and it is no wonder that the gardener's neighbors often ask for help in planning their own retreats.

ENGLAND, ITALY AND PROVENCE

The trend toward abundant summer bloom is generally perceived as an English influence. No one could deny that the Provençal garden today is being deeply affected by models from Britain, propagated not only by cosmopolitan gardeners but by the French gardening magazines which, although proposing regional types as well, offer soft and luscious images of misted English lawns and mixed borders to beginning gardeners of all climes.

Some conceptions of English gardening will always be doomed to failure in Provence, like that proposed by a homesick journalist, Lucinda Lambton. Traveling in the United States, she longed "not for vistas of formal refinement—which make me wince with displeasure as the trees, flowers and shrubs are strait-jacketed into the elegant fancies of their owners—but for a riotous array of blooms that bulge out into winding brick and grass paths, smother walls and arches and skip into ponds and streams . . . luscious and brilliant rooms. . . . " Great gardening traditions of the north have often derived from such a prodigal display. In a harsh Mediterranean climate, however, a "riotous array of blooms" could never seem "natural," or wild; it would inevitably be the effect of a guiding human hand. In the south, moreover, garden formalities do not mean making natural exuberance submit to "elegant fancies"; on the contrary, farmers know that pruning not only spurs plants to produce more fruit or flowers, but also that many suffer and die without this care. Gardens, like farms, were long ago accepted as

cerise-flowering cistus next to a stone bench. The narrow passage between the east and west terraces is one of the most successful areas: a stone trough built against the house is accented with flat box balls, while cerastium, dianthus and green santolina spill over above. Opposite, a low, ivy-clad wall shelters large balls of rosemary interspersed with cineraria and white lavender, fronted by small balls of alternating green and gray santolina. An old millstone mounted on the wall adds its own massive gray sphere. In the angle where this path meets the terrace, white-painted iron chairs sit sheltered by lilac, next to another lollipop, a flourishing white rose.

On the west side of the house lie two low rectangles outlined in cut stone that look like tapestries from the windows above: sages (including the red-leaved officinalis), thymes, dianthus, more boxwood. *Cynara cardunculus* (cardoon) creates a fountain of silver in contrast at the far end, hiding, along with other shrubs, the cutting garden. There is also a terrace running below the main garden where rows of mixed fruit trees stand among lavender lines—a clever echo of agricultural formalities which at the same time provides fruit for the gardener.

Mineral and plant elements constantly echo each other in this garden, in both color and form. All these small-scaled spaces are built from pale stone, and have slight differences of level that emphasize their individuality, just as each space has plants at different heights. Stone benches, walls, steps, containers, all repeat the elements of the landscape beyond, and their

*In Carpentras, a gardener
has imitated English models so successfully that a group of British visitors
exclaimed, "But this could be in England!"
to the great delight of their hostess. But her trellis with vine and
wisteria and her old stone well remain
unmistakably Provençal (above and opposite).*

"artificial" (oases, again), not designed to dominate the landscape but rather to coexist in hopeful, respectful complicity. Nor is Nature here normally "luscious" or "brilliant," but subtle and suggestive.

Starting from such differences in garden philosophy, some English gardeners in Provence have introduced the concept of a cultivated (often labor-intensive) wild garden—the Cameron garden at the Quatre Sources could, in part, be regarded as an example. Many, given the harmonious juxtaposition of farmland and wilderness common in Provence, simply include sections of the surrounding *garrigue* with its aromatics, evergreen shrubby plants, pines and oaks. But there is another aspect to wild gardening in the south: its English adepts are often conservationists for whom "natural" garden beauty, cultivated or simply preserved, must be protected against society's incursions. Hunters of all kinds, and peasants who cut down unproductive but beautiful trees, present a real threat.

One crusty Englishman takes pride in having created a rich collector's treasure trove on sandy, wooded land that no farmer would value. His peasant neighbors, who are also hunters every one, are the enemies of the wildlife he seeks to shelter. As for weeds, he says "what we get we pretend we want." But in spite of the garden's untamed look, it contains many rare, carefully imported items. Collections of rubus and rock roses, rare lilacs, mahonias, sorbus and maples nestle among the maritime pines, white and green oaks—all on two and one-half acres of land. Rosemary is a "natural"—but Miss Jessopp's upright is preferred. In shade, hellebores (*Helleborus orientalis* and *H. foetidus*) mixed with primulas with, in one moist spot, two camellias. Elsewhere, the six *Cyclamen neapolitanums* the owner brought from England have become, he boasts, six million, spread by ants. Vetch, *Euphorbia robbiae*, bergenias, wild campanula can be found in still other nooks.

This owner claims that French gardeners are unsympathetic to the subtleties of his "wild garden," preferring "splashy" colors and formal

lines. He recounts how, in front of a mass of white roses, a helpful neighbor said to him, "How sad, but you know you can graft red and orange ones onto them!" Set in a rather remote rural context, this very private garden is an unusual island, both blending and contrasting with local surroundings and traditions, full of the charm and eccentricities of its owner.

An L-shaped stone farmstead in the southern Alpilles recalls the wild garden insofar as the English owner has taken inspiration from the surrounding *garrigue*, which blends, surprisingly but fortuitously, with the models of Hidcote and Sissinghurst. It lies at the top of a gentle slope with rocky scrubland beyond, olive orchards behind and below, in one of the most dramatic of wild Provençal landscapes. The outer edge of the large, roughly rectangular garden consists of three separate promenades: first is the white walk, with its lilacs and iris, and *Photinia glabra*, a familiar from old Provençal farmsteads. The transition to the next stage is marked by a four-square grouping of pines sheltering an elegant Mycenean vase (copied from one at the British Museum). A left turn begins the bronze and red garden. One of the treasures of this section is the red-flowered *Buddleia colvilei* (buddleias of all kinds thrive here). A gnarled olive tree for foliage contrast stands in the middle.

The next left turn leads to the silver garden, highlighted with tones of apricot and pale yellow and white. The front margin is all "dusty miller" or cerastium, with a number of rare shrubs behind in tones of pale yellow and white (coronilla, *Olearia macrodonta*, *Lavatera* "Barnsley," shrubby germander and the much sought-after white poppy, *Romneya coulteri*). A *Clematis viticella* "Minuet" flows out over these shrubs and the hedge of *Buddleia alternifolia* behind; it is cut back after the first flowering of the coronillas. Across the path at the garden's southern edge lies a natural wildflower meadow full of poppies, mustard and wild campanulas, edged with formal shapes of dwarf Munstead lavender. Beyond this, across the lower olive orchard, the *garrigue* begins in earnest.

The garden's center, contained within this

The Petit Fontanille and the Jas Créma,
two of the region's most elaborate and successful recent creations,
both owe much to Anglo-Saxon influence.
And yet, each in its own way remains deeply attached to its
Provençal roots (opposite and following page).

tripartite walk, has two main sections: the first is an irregular space dominated by cistus, with a large, dusky-pink, spring-flowering tamarisk as a focal point, early pink iris at its feet. A grouping of wild cherries marks the southern edge, in bloom at the same time as the tamarisk. Their crests echo the billowing shapes of the hills beyond.

The second space is the garden's formal heart: a rosemary-enclosed rectangle around a fountain. Espaliered apples run along one side. The geometrical design does not shock here—the plantings it contains mirror the exuberance outside.

The owner calls this a "one pair of hands garden," all the more difficult to maintain since she is absent much of the winter and early spring. It is obvious however that she is trying to blend the best of England and Provence in a garden that makes many references to the traditions of both places. The *garrigue* has been made an active partner in the garden's design. One might call this a wild garden also because of the owner's search for a "natural" balance without chemicals of any kind, and in the protection she offers to spontaneous flora and fauna—even wild cats, a family of which has been welcome for generations. But at the same time, there are such rare treasures (so many more than can be mentioned here), such artful juxtapositions of garden plants with their rustic cousins, that this is also a place of considerable refinement.

English gardeners use plants that sometimes contrast strikingly with local vegetation. Red-

leaved foliage is perhaps the best example: wherever it appears, English inspiration is almost a certainty. Variegated foliage and blue conifers also come into play, and when well used, they simply extend the traditional Provençal themes beyond the grays and the blues of the *garrigue* plants. Even when new English foliage colors are introduced, they create new effects in the southern context: here stone is generally pale and luminous, in contrast to the lustrous, somber greens of box and laurustinus, *Quercus ilex*, the dusky tones of cedar and cypress—all of which can make a splendid foil for foliage variation. In the north, the mineral element is often dark, to be lightened by floral color.

British tradition also implies, even more importantly, a connoisseurship of plants which, often coupled with the collector's instinct, gives gardens far greater density of texture. Mr. Cameron and others whose properties have also been featured in books and magazines imported many of their favorite plants from Britain. Today (thanks in part to those same magazines), French nurseries supply an ever-increasing variety. Perhaps there have been some missed connections with local sources that actually can provide quite a number of uncommon plants. Surprisingly few gardeners know about the plant fair held every spring at the Château de Bellecoste between Arles and Nîmes, where many rare items can be found, though more and more enthusiasts are finding their way to Tarascon's flower festival.

The Jas Créma must stand as the senior and most famous of the English gardens in Provence.

Treasures from this bronze and red
garden in the Alpilles, which includes dark violet Salvia nemorosa, *luminous*
Berberis Barbarossa, *dusky* Cotinus coggygria, *brilliant*
crocosmia, and delicate Mrs. Oakley Fisher roses (top and above).
Today, inspiration for garden decor in Provence comes
from the four corners of the earth, as displayed by this Hungarian baptismal
font in the plains of the northern Alpilles (opposite).

It has everything—a dramatically wild mountain setting, outlying vineyards and orchards with strong agricultural geometries, a stunning view of the medieval village of Le Barroux dominated by a famous fortified keep, topiary, formal parterres, a secluded swimming pool, richly textured shrub and perennial borders, and fabulous collections of every conceivable sort. A vast, eighteenth-century farmstead (which was once a sheepfold, hence the name *jas*), presides without dominating, sheltering precious patio gardens under its wings.

The owner of this property, the Baroness de Waldner, spends much time in London. She has surrounded herself with mementos of her travels in India, including a wire-frame elephant clothed in yellow banksia roses and *Clematis balearica* majestically surveying the formal olive, lavender and rosemary-hedged parterre described earlier, and the similarly decked horses' heads that grace the upper entrance and the pool area. These unusual features fit very

well into this most personal and imaginative garden. It may be English in its careful texturing, and in the nurturing of rare plants—some hundred varieties of old roses, all fragrant, mix with shrubs and perennials outdoors, and there is a greenhouse well-stocked with even rarer treasures (a collection of passifloras, for example). It is Mediterranean, of course, in its cypresses, vineyards and olives, even more in its formalities.

Simple, modern, Gothic-inspired iron gates lead from the house past a hedge of Fantin-Latour roses to the protected, formal terraces below. The sloping beds on either side are filled with creeping ceanothus, acanthus, collections of iris and narcissus, hellebores, iberis, sages, solanums. . . . Here the garden's main reservoir is overhung by a Cecile Brunner rose and pink wisteria. In this corner are more rare roses: *Rosa roxburghii*, *R. viridiflora* and a deep red Etoile d'Hollande.

In the garden's heart lie two rectangular ter-

*The colors of the Jas Créma are soft
but rich, never blatant but not overly pale, either. They include yellows
and apricots, and show that much
careful thought has gone into their combining.*

races sheltered by high walls to the east and west, bordered by their own retaining walls toward the south and by the house itself at the top, north level. These are both planted in a pattern of squares and rectangles that has been carefully designed to avoid complete symmetry. The design is never monotonous, and the plantings are full of happy surprises.

The dark, evergreen squares that deck these two main levels are made from low pittosporum hedging. On the upper one, they surround four box towers, while the seven lower squares enclose pillared roses (Félicité Perpétue). Within these blocks, one or at the most two plants provide a dominant color on the ground: catnip, pale pink verbena, agapanthus, cerise dianthus, blue fescue, an artemisia and gray santolina around the roses; white oxalis, red oxalis, deep pink verbena, and agapanthus for the box towers. This is the most formal and central part of the garden.

Around these geometries, much delicate detail softens the effect. The retaining wall that separates the two levels is planted with *Cheiranthus* "Bowles" hybrid alternating with *Cinerarea* "White Diamond" (allowed to flower since it has white and not yellow blooms). Punctuated by white Swany roses, this mixture of spring blossoms makes a sumptuously cascading line.

On these two terraces, narrow paths run at right angles, themselves edged with imaginative borders like embroidered hems: in one spot, two colors of agapanthus alternate, the blue underplanted with white alyssum, the white with blue felicia. In early spring, before the

alyssum is sown, pansies fill the space around the emerging, sword-like leaves. The most spectacular edge, however, consists of pink Nozomi roses trained on low hoops, their tiny, pale flowers in delicate contrast with the dark pittosporum behind.

When starting this garden, Madame de Waldner first had the terraces built, then outlined her plan in white powder to judge the effect. It can all be seen from the windows of the residence above. She felt that strong southern light needed stronger lines than in the gardens she had created under northern skies. At the same time, however, she wanted a garden suitable for strolling. Paths about sixty centimeters wide and obviously well traveled connect every corner. And in spite of the sense of enclosure conveyed by the geometrical heart, its outer limits graciously meet the surrounding fields of olives, vines, and cherry orchards, whose careful pruning repeats the spirit of the inner garden. A row of five cherries at the southeastern edge, for example, has been carefully ordered with the tallest in the middle, to form a gently arched line. On the west side of the house, single cherry trees with New Dawn climbing through them, single olives with circles of irises at their feet, provide a link to the orchards beyond. Shrubby germander (*Teucrium fruticans*) has been pruned into a smooth gray ring at the foot of some trees to good effect. At its southern boundary, the garden is protected from the road below by a tall cypress hedge. Every section allows a view of the hilltown and its castle rising opposite.

*Nestled into a corner of the Jas Créma
is a walled herb garden whose nine boxwood rectangles surround beds of
Green Diamond rose, tarragon, marjoram, chives, mint,
sage with white camassia, and rosemary. Cypresses, planted in buried pots
to keep them miniature, stand in the center of each (top).
The Jas Créma also makes fine use of sculptural foliage like that of the typically
Mediterranean acanthus, here in bud (above).*

The name of this property, Jas Créma, means a burnt sheepfold, and suggests a scene of desolation that could hardly be imagined today. This garden's beginnings were not auspicious, however, and its history bears witness to Madame de Waldner's imagination and determination. When she first fell in love with the site in the late 1970s, the property was not for sale. After a difficult acquisition, and while truckloads of precious plants were already arriving, she discovered that there was no source of water. Numerous efforts to locate a former spring proved to no avail, but finally a second diviner found the right spot to drill. Today the garden is an oasis of flowering and fruitfulness.

The Petit Fontanille garden at the western end of the Alpilles, well-known in both England and America, is often considered the most English of the neo-Provençal gardens. It came into existence because its owner, former ambassador Ann Cox Chambers, was moved by the blending of wild and rural landscapes to imagine a "romantic garden-in-nature." The property lies totally unsuspected off a rural road, its access leading through fields and vineyards, with wilder spaces full of bright yellow *Spartium junceum* in the spring. The vines were planted in a number of varieties with the advice of a vintner neighbor, and the estate has its own label.

After contemplating the site's special needs, Mrs. Cox Chambers invited English designer Peter Coates to advise her, and says that he created the garden's basic structure. His presence may still be felt in the mixing of red and variegated foliage plants that is stronger here than anywhere else. Many friends have contributed since, including Mr. Cameron of the Quatre Sources, English expert Rosemary Verey, and Mr. Gainey, the aforementioned American garden designer. The result is a sophisticated, labor-intensive garden that gets all the ample care it deserves—including copious watering. Mrs. Cox Chambers remains the guiding spirit, orchestrating and directing; but she is also a keen gardener who likes to do some of her own digging and planting.

In the beginning there was a seventeenth and nineteenth-century *mas*. There were fields of lavender and rosemary, a wonderful avenue of cypress, good shade trees (the thick dome of a hackberry, the lighter, feathery foliage of sophora and gleditsia), odd ornamental elements like a patch of *Yucca gloriosa*, a trellis with roses, and the twin cherry laurels by the front door whose feet Peter Coates enclosed in wooden casing, so they would seem to be growing in Versailles tubs. Today the traditional rectangular terrace in front of the farmstead has been miraculously transformed (with the magic that is water) into a curving greensward. It is now broken by flagstones to and from the white stone steps that lead to the parking areas and the tennis courts beyond.

From the top of these steps, the house lies to the right and the main garden area to the left. The major axis of the latter is a double row of the original cypresses (known familiarly as the "Grande Allée"). It slopes up toward a distant obelisk, beyond a rise of grassy, stone steps. To the left, another, less formal lane (forming a V with the first) also leads upward. Plantings here, still against the cypress wall, mix an impressive range of colors and textures: Russian olive (*Elaeagnus angustifolia*), oleander, purple plum, laurustinus, purple lilacs, ceanothus, *Cotoneaster lacteus*, ornamental apple, crape myrtles, and even eucalyptus. Here are some of Peter Coates's red and yellow foliage plants: as ground covers, yellow oregano, purple ajugas and podagraria (which he describes as a variegated, non-spreading ground elder). A particularly gray Russian olive overshadowing a red-leaved *Berberis thunbergii* marks a focal point in the path.

Both the Grande Allée and the informal lane to its left lead up to a plateau where the swimming pool, invisible from the house, extends its formal expanse of soft blue. At its east end stands a seven-sided, seventeenth-century stone *folie* serving as a pool shelter. This was brought from a château in the Gard and can be glimpsed from all over the garden. Pots of oleander, citrus and white annuals surround it, and with silver foliage create a magical effect, especially at night.

*At the Petit Fontanille,
the main perspective leads toward an obelisk. Oleanders and lilacs peek
through the evergreen curtains underplanted
with rosemary, myosotis (a particularly pale, natural-looking variety)
and White Triumphant tulips.*

The pool is backed by a high wooded bank that marks the garden's south limit, and directs the eye to the open crowns of thousand-year-old olive trees at the far end. These and the strip of lawn surrounding them lead toward a carefully cultivated though natural-looking wildflower meadow, where many annuals and biennials (cosmos, coreopsis, thistles, single gypsophilia, larkspur, cornflowers, nemophila) stand among the grasses. American Queen Anne's lace and Stone River mountain daisy from Georgia have been imported by Mr. Gainey to create an expanse that is continually in flower. Cypress and a spreading fig frame the view on the north side.

Back by the house, to the right of the Grande Allée, a giant hackberry shades an elegant stone table and benches. Immediately beyond is the most formal area of the garden: a box parterre filled with English roses around topiary olives like four great globes. Stopping the perspective at the south end is a rose arbor of stone columns and a lattice roof from which tumbles the climbing rose Clair Matin. A circular pond in the same axis concentrates color (always muted here) in the pale pink and white petunias and the Swan River daisies that encircle it.

A second garden level lies below this main area, to the west. There are several ways down that focus on an intriguing, semi-circular fountain, with lions and water lilies, backed against the retaining wall. Beyond, two large fields of lavender flank a rectangle of arborescent rosemaries, limited in the distance by a laurel hedge. At the extreme western limit, visible from the main level, can be glimpsed one of the property's most prized areas: a cutting garden and *potager*. The first was designed by Gainey, the second by Verey, both taking inspiration from seventeenth-century sources.

The vegetable plot is planted in a floral daisy design, low box and santolina hedges forming the petals. At the four corners are standard topiary lonicera, and in each bed stands a pyra-

Cypresses punctuate every section of the Petit Fontanille garden — slim and spreading, both massive and small-scaled. A guest once suggested that her hostess must count cypresses to fall asleep!

mid planted with tomatoes. Here grow ornamental cabbages, nasturtiums, angelica, several varieties of lettuces, chives, double chamomile, and other plants. This space provides, among other things, Alpine strawberries for the owner's breakfast, nasturtiums and mixed greens for her salads. What is more, the domain produces its own honey, wine and olive oil, thus proving that even neo-Provençal gardens can cater to the palate.

The cutting garden, reminiscent of Barnsley House, has teak benches at each end and more linear plantings: artemisias, roses, variegated pittosporum, nepetas, zinnias, cleomes. The path between the two rectangles that prolongs the main east-west axis of the garden ends in the old threshing circle, where cypresses and a young hackberry frame the view beyond.

These are but some of the extensions of this complex garden. Delightful smaller spaces are found around the house itself, including a small back garden on the north side. Here blue and

white ceramic pots find their colors echoed, along with violet, in the tumbling plants around them. These patio areas are all encircled by pots at various levels, spilling over with pale bloom. The house walls are not neglected: vines, creepers, trachelospermum and a rarer fremontodendron climb happily.

This is a garden where care is taken to ensure fragrance, and moonflowers are grown especially for the owner's private terrace. Much attention has also been paid to sculpture and containers. Stone urns with flame tops frame the patio by the main entrance and are matched by larger urns of the same design at the other end of the Grande Allée. Statues emerge from foliage here and there, framed by pencil cypresses or olive globes, as well as more free-flowing forms like a corkscrew willow.

Like all great gardens, this one is in constant evolution. Mrs. Cox Chambers remains enchanted with the spirit of place that first inspired her. A new area has just been developed to the

*The shaded seating area around the front
door of the Petit Fontanille contains a rich array of pots and wall plants
and elegant nineteenth-century cast-iron furniture;
to the west, a dining platform raised like a stage is sheltered by the canopy of two
Sophora japonica edged with Iceberg roses.*

left: a large rectangle once again, with a slightly sunken winter garden. The shape and proportions of this impressive stone structure, which looks as if it has always been there, echo those of the pool house above. Its farthest wall was built first, as a series of wooden trellis-work arches, left like a stage awaiting its actors while its destiny was being decided. Now that it has been enclosed in the winter garden, it provides a protective backdrop for tender treasures and a fascinating collection of rare garden furniture.

The general style of this garden might be described as a constant interplay between formal shapes and flowing lines, with a great deal of attention paid to textural detailing in even the smallest spaces. Advisor Gainey has followed Mrs. Cox Chamber's lead in looking for "romance" in his designs: pointing out the *Clematis montana* "Rubens" climbing through a cypress, he exclaims: "That's Veronica's veil," describing the artemisias at its foot as "her tears." But he is all common sense when it comes to the garden's mixture of trees, shrubs, perennials and annuals ("bedding in, not bedding out," he says). Good companion planting is for him the secret of this garden's success. Each group must be integrated and natural-looking, and pansies, even if pale, may still be too reminiscent of the public garden. Here as elsewhere, he likes to try out associations as bouquets before planting; for example, purple plum foliage with yellow banksia rose sprays, lilac blossoms and deep red-flowered weigela.

For Mr. Gainey, this is very much a Provençal garden, because of its integration into the surrounding landscape—although it certainly stands as one of the most self-contained examples current, where even the view is far less interesting than the garden itself. The outlying areas are planned and planted, certainly, but not visible from the garden's heart as at the Jas Créma. Of course, the predominance of cypress and olive trees immediately gives it a Mediterranean feel. Rosemary Verey, asked if this was a Provençal garden, looked around her and said that it was southern because everything flowers so much earlier here. And certain-

ly this affects the balance of the garden's design, its associations and evolution throughout the seasons. But she felt that apart from the olive trees, the scene before her could be in England. Other parts of the garden, perhaps the northern courtyard door flanked by its pots, have more of an American feel. The design contains, on the whole, too much formality to be only English, and yet there is nothing here of the French parterre, rather a southern sense of foliage and forms. This is surely the most cosmopolitan garden of the new school, and a synthesis of the best that can be had on two continents.

English influence in Provence cannot seek to reproduce the luxuriant summer exuberance of its inspiration; but it can and does mean an emphasis on texture as well as design, the collector's instinct pushed to a passion, an extension of the range of foliage colors, and even the inclusion of far more roses. There is also a concern for breaking up spaces—and colors—into areas of specialization, beyond those that seasonal variation and food production have always dictated. At its best, English gardening in Provence also means an imaginative use of native plants, a deep respect for southern style and for the spirit of place, wherever this may be.

One astonishing example is the golf course at Les Baux: nowhere would north and south seem more irreconcilable than in such a project, especially one set amid the gaunt and tortured crags of this famous valley. But British landscapers with local guidance have produced a small miracle, where nature is tamed but not forced. Today at the Golf des Baux, the greens nestle among the grays, players move among olive orchards and rocky outcroppings that are part of one great, highly successful, Anglo-Provençal garden.

England certainly leads the fashion in gardens today. But Provence has kept its deep ties with Italy, and some modern owners and landscapers look south rather than north for their models. Not far from Le Petit Fontanille, equally unsuspected by the passing motorist, lies another property that, with its neighbor, was once part of the same territory near a large spring in

*Climbing to the main lawn of the Petit Fontanille,
one comes upon a shaded knot garden enclosed by cypresses and laurel
hedging on three sides. This beautiful,
small-scaled plot was designed by Rory Cameron.*

the Alpilles. The larger domain also began as a farmhouse, but was transformed into a château in the late eighteenth and early nineteenth century. Its architecture was revamped in the Italian style, and formal gardens spread around it on several levels. After a long period of neglect, it has been purchased by a German couple intent on restoring its Mediterranean elegance. The gardens are being remodeled by a talented local designer, Dominique Lafourcade (helped by nurseryman Bernard Clareton). Her inspiration remains Mediterranean.

The long approach road (unfortunately rather suburban in its paving) passes through wild landscapes mixed with vineyards. Movement is uphill from here, along intricate, elegant ramps and terraces. The house lies at a diagonal to the hillside rising south, and all the gardens, with their strict internal geometries, form a gentle curve around the building. The rhythms thus created are exceptional, the forms always held tensely off-center in their gradual ascent, set off by the steep *garrigue* hillside that borders the property to the east and west of this narrow valley.

The heart of this garden, which the house terrace overlooks, is the lowest, largest and most formal part, and the first encountered on arrival: a large rectangular Italian water garden, with patterns of yews and cypresses around canals and basins. The stone columns of its pergola run along its east side, fragrance wafting up to the onlookers at the balustrade above. A smaller and lower parterre called the boxwood (or Provençal) garden lies further up, its patterns filled in with colored sand. On the third level up is a kind of wild garden, still contained within a rectangle, where thickets and groves of evergreens set off crape myrtles, and mixed ground covers (vinca, lamium, et cetera) add density of texture. A formal flight of steps leads to the top level, where agriculture and garden geometries mix: ancient olive trees border a vineyard cut in half by a long rustic pergola in the axis of the steps. Table grapes have been trained to cover it in such a way that thirsty strollers may seek both shade and sustenance. Beyond lies the mountain itself.

All these levels are visible from windows on the southwest and northwest sides of the house. But the buildings themselves are set on a sort of pedestal composed of smaller, irregular terraces, more intimate garden spaces. There is the rose arbor, and the exotic garden with its outer wisteria wall overhanging the Provençal parterre. All spaces are outlined by cut-stone retaining walls, arches, balustrades, steps, and they shelter stone basins and fountains. A new area is being developed behind the house, around a swimming pool planted with simple groups of Mediterranean plantings.

This elegant garden is above all architectural, by the beauty of its retaining walls, the complexity of its terracing that surrounds and displays the château, by its multiple views that allow the stroller to keep rediscovering the ensemble, and by the careful insertion of its formal lines and spaces into a particularly wild setting. Sculpture is not more important here than in the Petit Fontanille, but it is used differently—as part of the architectural whole rather than as accents for the vegetation. Water is treated in a similar fashion: it is part of a succession of basins and fountains, a special focus for the general design. Texture is every bit as important here as in the English model, but its value comes from the juxtaposition of water, sparkling or reflecting, with pale stone and dark, generally evergreen foliage, rather than from the happy marriage, for instance, of a rare pale columbine and a dark velvety rose. Not that flowers are absent, far from it, but they never predominate.

English influence, Italian inspiration: foreign models are once again useful today because of societal changes that are not unlike those of past centuries. Many gardens in Provence are now being designed for a wealthy and cosmopolitan elite that admires the elegance of local country architecture but wants, in restoring a farmhouse, for example, something more prestigious than a working farm. Provence appeals precisely because it has traditionally blended château and farm in a variety of ways—after all, ambitious owners have been transforming agricultural properties into lordly residences since the Renaissance. Most neo-Provençal gardeners today want to start from a farm property, however; they find in Provençal château gardens little scope for modern taste, with their broadleafed, evergreen-layered woods, or their steep terracing supported by cut-stone retaining walls. In modifying a more rustic property, many choose simply to enrich it with English borders, and their success depends largely on how well-integrated, both practically and esthetically, these are to the Provençal setting. Other owners resort to professional landscaping, which in its most facile form means uniform gardens all planted with the same cypresses, olive trees, oleanders and lawns. Young landscapers with more imagination are clearly looking for more ambitious models, but seem to be floundering among the variety of foreign choices available. Few have had the chance to visit old Provençal gardens and form their own ideas of local traditions. Working for a demanding cosmopolitan public that wants gardens of some prestige,

professional garden designers can find the entire issue of models confusing.

Dominique Lafourcade and her husband, an interior designer, have found a solution to the conflicting demands of this new public in a style that she calls Italianate. Perhaps it would be fairer to say that Italian villa gardens rather than Provençal château parks have provided her with inspiration for enlarging the local agrarian tradition, but the result is an essentially Mediterranean blend in which the latter plays as large a part as the former. This couple's own, recently purchased farmstead provides an excellent example. Set among flat fields and pasture land near Saint-Rémy, it drew their attention first by the stately row of ancient oaks to the north, and magnificent plane trees to the south.

The old farmstead itself was transformed first: the middle section was raised to create a center with two wings of equal dimensions; windows were redesigned to be more consistent in size, and arranged symmetrically on the long façade. Thus the irregularities of peasant architecture were ordered in a more château-like manner. Beautiful old tiles replaced the dirt floors. Carved stone doors and other elegant detailing have added nobility to the general aspect.

What then of the garden? Close by the old farmstead stood a huge metallic shed, which was promptly dismantled. Its cement foundations became the support for a rectangular basin into which water now flows from a raised fountain at one end. The majestic shade trees on both sides of the house were restored to new health. And then the designing began in earnest. The Provençal farmstead elements have not been rejected, but a richer plan was wanted, in keeping with the new elegance of the buildings themselves.

Madame Lafourcade, working with a large, flat, windswept space, designed a formal layout where shaded enclosures and long pergolas alternate with open vistas; where water clearly links the different parts; where strong design does not exclude complex texture, but foliage shape and color clearly dominate floral

Edith Wharton wrote, "Though it is an exaggeration to say that there are no flowers in Italian gardens, yet to enjoy and appreciate the Italian garden-craft one must always bear in mind that it is independent of floriculture." Contemporary creations like this Alpilles property still observe the custom.

elements. She has carefully avoided too much pretension by choosing only local plants for the large blocks, those commonly found around farmsteads, in château gardens and the *garrigue*: box, laurels and laurustinus, olive trees—the latter not in the ground but in terracotta urns lining the main canal. Two rectangles of lavender extend the symmetry of the design to the garden's outer limits, where a natural pond, surrounded by wild suckering wicker with its bright yellow winter wood, links garden to landscape.

Two long vine and roseclad arbors extend from the house limits to mark the garden's boundaries east and west. Centered between the two lies the main basin with its canal (edged near the house with the olive urns, in the distance with the simple, furry gray of *Stachys lanata*). A formal parterre of carefully pruned multileveled laurustinus, a simple form of topiary, echoes the château tradition to the east of the canal; to the west lies an enclosed Italianate

parterre, one entire wall of which is composed of ancient vinestock. A cypress walk leads from this square to a spreading mulberry plane, the whole enclosed in fragrant laurel, in striking contrast with the open spaces outside.

There is as yet no swimming pool. If one is constructed later, it will be at the western end of the house, protected by a double, semi-circular cypress hedge. The pool will repeat this half-moon shape, linked to the building by a complex pergola. The corresponding space at the east end of the house will become a decorative vegetable garden. Throughout the design, within the walled garden or in sheltered nooks by the house, floral accents allow for collections of rarer plants, now being established. Thus are rural traditions, modern comfort and the elegance of a new synthesis felicitously combined.

It is obvious from these examples that many of the best neo-Provençal gardens have been created by gifted amateurs. Like the professionals, and like the designers of centuries past,

*The formalities of this Italianate garden are softened
by the magnificent cypresses and a gigantic white poplar (above). The Provençal or box garden
of this Alpilles property is filled with colored sand and backed by the wild
hillside of this narrow valley (opposite). A fine old mas has been transformed by the Lafourcades
into the focal point of an elaborate garden plan, created for the most
part with simple, local plants. Olive trees form an avenue along the canal leading
from the house (following page).*

they look beyond their boundaries for inspiration. Some have been inspired by the formal Mediterranean agricultural model in which the human hand both tames and nurtures, imposing form as one educates a child; others seek an artful concentration of surrounding wilderness; still others impose upon the land and climate a vision that "forces nature" in the regal, northern style. The gardener's dream must always confront the realities of climate and soil, which restrict newcomers and natives alike. But there are gardens belonging to old Provençal families that are full of camellias and rhododendrons—these owners have no need to prove anything, and can give themselves up to an idiosyncratic vision that no northener would dare attempt. The question of models, local or foreign, is only part of a much larger question: stylistic authenticity. This issue takes on greater importance as more and more gardens, both professional and private, are created all over Provence today.

*A 1900s wood nymph is framed
by dark foliage in the Italian-style château garden. The Lafourcades restored
their farmhouse by making its lines more symmetrical.
The canal leading to the garden's outlying areas is edged quite simply
with santolina and* Stachys lanata *(opposite).*

GROWING THE "ORTHENTIC"

In his famous novel about rural Provence, *Jean de Florette*, Marcel Pagnol wrote about city people repossessing an old family farm. Meeting up with the neighboring peasant, the hero explains that he wants "to eat the vegetables of my garden, the oil of my olive trees, to suck the fresh eggs of my chickens, to get drunk on the wine of my vines, and as far as possible to eat the bread I make with my wheat." He has come, he insists, "to cultivate the authentic." The neighbor, Ugolin, recounts all this to his sly old uncle, Papet—both are determined to trick the newcomer out of his land. The latter asks what the city man plans to grow and Ugolin replies: "Vegetables, vines, wheat, and above all, he said, he's going to 'cultivate the orthentic'! Orthentics everywhere! What are they"? Says the uncle: "It must be a plant that grows in books. . . . "

It is certainly a plant that grows in dreams. The hero's vision is easily recognizable as the ancient Roman ideal that has so deeply affected agriculture—and gardens—in Provence. Jean de Florette too brought plants from faraway places, and tried fabulous innovations.

How is the Provençal gardener today to grow "orthentics" in his plot, mountain or valley, château park, farmyard, village or city courtyard? Here as in other contexts, authenticity involves integration of a past heritage. Gardening traditions exist in Provence but are not generally well-known, even locally. What is ubiquitous, however, is a nostalgic vision of pre-industrial rural life—one with proven commercial appeal to the outside world. "Old-time" Provence appears picturesque to the charmed and willing eye. Provençal farms and villages seem both ancient and ageless to visitors and settlers, while their original inhabitants are often torn between encouraging the quaintness so beloved of tourists, and insisting on their right to participate in the modern world. Even the most sensitive outsiders are tempted to superimpose on Provence the dream that has seduced their imaginations: Van Gogh sought a Japanese "simplicity of nature" here, and gave trees and roofs a Gothic twist.

The past is still alive in Provence, of course,

though for modern agriculture this is both a blessing and a burden. This part of the lower Rhône valley has the highest productivity per acre and the most expensive agricultural labor force in the country. Mediterranean farming, say the experts, necessitates highly specialized skills—and the devotion of those who know each plant as if it were their own child. Fortunately, farming is still much in evidence. Anywhere in this heart of Provence except on the freeways your car may be stopped by a flock of sheep. Failing that, you will certainly find yourself behind a thresher, or a tractor drawing a huge vat of just-harvested grapes. Nevertheless, faced with international competition, farmers are changing millenia-old techniques. Skilled, intensive, highly personal labor once produced beautiful objects created with the simplest of materials, worked with care for immediate, practical purposes; now these objects are sold in antique shops, having been made obsolete by modern machinery. In furnishings as in plantings, newcomers often choose fragments they find decorative, without always understanding the logic that once gave them value. A beauty that was closely linked to function, to the cycle of seasons, to the growth of both landscape and the people who lived in it has given way to ornamental decor. Newcomers often re-create the rural past, says Jean-Robert Pitte in his history of the French landscape, much as the Romantics re-created the Middle Ages—theatrically and carelessly, in purely sentimental homage.

The problems that sometimes oppose natives and newcomers (inhabitants and residents, as geographers say) are familiar: they latter may buy land at prices higher than locals can afford, close off rights of way, draw water for gardens and swimming pools. It is above all the new settlers who have given far greater place to purely ornamental gardening, and this emphasis may be one of their more profound effects. But while this trend may be viewed negatively—the landscape as mere picturesque scenery—it can also be an enrichment. Sometimes outsiders can help natives appreciate what has always been taken for granted,

Plant connotations play a crucial role in determining garden style. For many people, both natives and newcomers, olive trees and lavender signify Provence. But in traditional southern gardens, laurustinus, box and acanthus are much more common.

and help them find beauty even in the "useless."

Communication is not always easy. Pagnol, again in *Jean de Florette*, imagined a wonderful misunderstanding on the subject of garden beauty (with his usual compassion for both sides). To discourage the city people from settling, not only does the farmer plug up the spring, but he tries to create a scene that will frighten and rebuff them. He sows handfuls of thistles and wild clematis seeds, pruning the brambles to strengthen them, even taking cuttings and graftings of dog roses to make the site as inhospitable and unproductive as possible. He revels in his evil intentions, calling himself "the devil's peasant." But when the city folks arrive, they stare amazed at the beauty of the landscape thus created, calling it (what else?) an "earthly paradise." The wife, a former opera singer, begins to make bouquets.

The future of gardens in Provence must be a synthesis of local and imported elements. Authenticity first means recognizing a past that has been largely underestimated, acknowledging the roles played throughout history by both local conditions and foreign models. From that basis, one can pose questions about innovation—which are largely unanswerable, no doubt, but important to ask. Penelope Hobhouse aptly expresses in her book *Garden Style* the ideal rapport between individual initiative and custom, which must entail "some sort of reconciliation between a love of plants and the creation of an art form where plants and architecture together make an integrated unit. . . . Knowledge and appreciation of garden history become

a background 'grammar' to personal gardening ideals."

Specific problems arise. What, for example, are the dangers involved in transposing traditional elements onto a new setting that may seem to work against their original logic: lavender fields from mountain to valley, olive trees from *garrigue* to lawn? Should a boxwood labyrinth like those of the Aix country bastides be set in front of a rugged hilltop farmhouse? Should a terraced garden be created on the virgin slopes of the Alpilles, where this type of construction has never existed? Each section of the country has its microclimates, each has had its particular evolution. If we mix and match, are we creating pastiche, or is this the legitimate innovation of a new style?

Similar problems arise with plant connotations. In a recent controversy over an ancient poplar tree destined to be sacrificed in the renovation of a well-loved public garden, the architects defended this step on the grounds that the poplar is "not a noble essence." While there may be other, practical reasons to justify their decision, the issue of nobility set the cat among the pigeons, precisely because it seems a criterion appropriate for the Ile-de-France and not Provence. Even the current transformations of old farmsteads into prestigious residences risk evoking the *ferme ornée* of Marie-Antoinette rather than the local spirit of the château-farm. As Mme. Lafourcade shows us, the difference can lie in the cultural associations of the plants selected. Surprisingly, perhaps, the two most common plants in traditional Provençal gardens are laurustinus and acanthus, not lavender. Gray santolina has also become prolific.

The importation of plants from other climates often causes similar dilemmas, even when, as quite frequently happens, they flourish in their new home. Plant suppliers in the south are constantly updating and enlarging their selections, now that (largely due to foreign influence) the public is ever more attuned and informed. But do red-foliage plants and yellow conifers "belong" in Provence? Much depends on how they are used. Certainly a rock garden planted among large, rough-hewn boulders in

In contemporary gardens, gray-leaved santolina occurs much more frequently than lavender.

an area famous for its beautifully tailored, dry-set stone terracing strikes a false note; and when it is decked out in miniature multicolored conifers and weeping trees of all description, it shocks rather than pleases the viewer (although presumably it delights its owner?). Gardeners wishing to be safe imitate the plants growing wild on their land when they begin—and what a range can be found in just the achilleas and sages!

Plant connotations cause endless problems: are birch trees too northern? More appropriate for mountain than valley settings? Olivier de Serres grew them in the Midi in the sixteenth century. Is historical precedent justification? Broadleafed evergreens raise similar issues: the *garrigue* is rich with these plants whose growth patterns fit the local climate, but now that the choice has been enriched by imports, why do many gardeners welcome choisya and ceanothus, but reject escallonia and cotoneasters as unsuitably northern or park-like? The conifers

are complicated too: Arizona cypresses, by their color alone, seem false in many contexts, unless perhaps they grow irregularly near wild conifers of the same hue. And now that they serve as hedging for identical suburban villas all over France, they evoke the danger of arbitrary plantings without regional roots, poor integration into the landscape—in a word, poor taste. The question of taste is even thornier than that of authenticity, and will be left suspended here. But the extremes of incoherence and uniformity both represent real threats.

One essential element of the Provençal garden tradition is very much with us today: its emphasis on the production and enjoyment of food. Today, the many foreigners who flock to Provence are seeking some total vision of "the good life." Gardening is an important source of this evocative earthiness, all the more so because, in the south, it has traditionaily catered not only to visual effect but also to taste, smell, and even feel.

One could imagine a garden composed entirely of different thymes—from wild thymes to more domesticated ones—as well as for different times of day and different fragrances.

Hotels and restaurants in Provence naturally make the most of this heritage. A few, like the Oustau de Baumanière, grow most of their own vegetables and herbs. The best always feature a garden patio, perhaps inspired by the delightful shade of old farmstead terraces. The Priory in Villeneuve-les-Avignon also has an extended garden for strolling, adapted to the requirements of summer visitors with its constant bloom. But though the main rectangular plot was re-landscaped only a few years ago by François Deieu, its setting dates back to the fourteenth century. Remodeled in later centuries, the property was turned into an elegant hotel (run by the same family as today) in the 1930s. A pergola that provides the main path from hotel to parking lot beyond is covered with roses that were planted just after the war (the single-blossomed red climber found in many local gardens). In the formal area to the right, box-edged paths and circles surround Anduze pots, but some of the lines are lost in the riot of flowers that prosper throughout the growing season. Against the protected far wall is a typical Provençal arbor with stone columns and ancient wisteria. All this is visible from the sheltered dining terrace, where products of the local *terroir*, transformed with refinement by chef Serge Chenet, are served to lucky diners.

Provençal cooking is famous for its aromatics, but where, outsiders often ask, are the herb gardens of Provence? In this respect more than ever, the entire landscape may be seen as a garden. The rocky, exposed *garrigue* soil produces concentrated essences in its many thymes,

savories, sages, fennel, rosemary, and the sunshine intensifies these even further. Damper areas provide wild parsley (flat-leafed or Italian, as it is otherwise called) and mint—the latter blended with almonds, fennel and anchovies makes an ambrosial paste called *sassoun*, which is spread on bread. Annual herbs that need water, like basil, are cultivated as part of the plot near the kitchen door, or among the vegetables that it meets again in the famous *pistou* (basil) soup. But the conception of a separate garden for herbs, in particular one with any kind of formal organization, remains foreign.

Today, however, two unusual botanical gardens present a rich variety of aromatics, among other *garrigue* plants, all labeled for easy identification. One is the old farmstead that was once the home of entomologist Henri Fabre, at Sérignan-le-Comtat north of Orange. This extraordinary scholar and collector is so admired by Japanese visitors that the entire property was almost shipped to Japan. . . . Luckily for the local heritage, the *harmas*, or wild land, that Fabre first used as a scouting terrain for insects has been left whole. After his death it was transformed into a delightful garden, where on Wednesday afternoons schoolteachers may be found sitting under an ancient oak, reading Fabre's instructive tales for children to their pupils, while the many small sounds and fragrances of the garden float by.

The other is a public garden in Nyons, a town famous for its olives and oil; here a dedicated pair of herbalists have organized, by plant families and by use, riverside terraces around a

*At the old Prieuré hotel in Villeneuve,
a recently planted parterre of summer flowers is surrounded by an ancient
Wisteria sinensis growing on an elegant stone pergola,
and an arch of roses planted just after World War II (above and opposite).*

1900-style distillery. Two varieties of lavender, aspic and vera, logically flank their sterile, commercially desirable hybrid. Sages, umbellifers, junipers, roses are here in abundance. Large trees, including limes and a five-hundred-year-old olive, provide shade for pleasant and aromatic walking, or lingering on one of the three stone benches. A sculpture called *Tree of Life* by a local artist, Gaudefroy, pays homage to the garden's inspiration.

One section of this garden has medicinal plants, another those used for the distillation of perfumes, yet another culinary herbs. There are now one hundred and eighty varieties with some three hundred anticipated. Here gardeners can learn to recognize local flora as well as introduced species, and there are some interesting experiments as well: a bed of *Rosa gallica* underplanted with a "lawn" of wild achillea and dichondra.

Aromatics are attracting more and more attention as an extension of the traditional production of plant essences for perfume. A fascinating book, *Le Nez de la Drome* by Anne Simonet and Jean Lenoir, even includes small flasks of many local essences for sniffing: peach, olive oil, lime flower . . . even goat cheese!

Rare is the Provençal garden that contains nothing edible: even if the olive trees do not bear, there is usually a fruit tree in one corner or another. Some gardeners have taken special pains to create unusual effects, like the elegant but rustic lane of mixed fruit and olive trees bordered by chrysanthemums described earlier. Rarer are those who go to the trouble of maintaining a vegetable garden, with its constant demands and periods of unlovely transition. Peasant gardens of course still thrive, and so do the château plots of vegetables behind high walls—their owners may nowadays look at them with fresh admiration.

Occasionally, however, an inventive gardener working within these traditions produces a splendidly decorative plot of vegetables. Even modern creations remain formal, however; they are never the free-form invasion of one realm by another, nor an exuberant, all-inclusive profusion of color, texture and fragrance. The local

practice of growing tomatoes on bamboo stakes in pairs, crossing at regular intervals along a single long support, provides a strong structural feature that may be echoed by artichokes (this region is famous for the small violet ones), zucchini and pumpkin plants (both important ingredients in Provençal cooking), grown among espaliered trees. Hollyhocks and dahlias accentuate the larger scale of these impressive plots, and of course there are roses. The traditional cutting garden contributes to the decor. Even the cardoon so often grown in England for its formal stature has long been a source of food in Provence: cardoon stalks in anchovy sauce are served in many households on Christmas Eve.

By far the best of the modern, decorative kitchen gardens belongs to the elaborate property of Val Joanis, a wine château between Aix and the Luberon. In fact, this property is in itself a compendium of the Provençal garden, old and new. It belongs to a local family, and Madame Cecile Chancel is responsible for the magnificent recent creations.

The buildings are situated on a rise in the middle of a valley full of vineyards and more recently planted olive orchards, protected on the north and west by a wild wood of green oaks and Aleppo pines. The house itself is simple, a cross between an Aix bastide, a mountain château and a large, seigneurial farmstead. The owner points out that even the proportions of its windows bear witness to this blending, too wide for the fortified style, but narrower than those of the secure suburban estate. Its walls are covered with a sandy wash, though bare stone

*Herb gardens are not traditional in Provence,
where the wild garrigue provides such a profusion; but a few botanical gardens
like the one in Nyons have planted and labeled aromatics
for easy identification. Here are the gray and green santolinas that are
so often juxtaposed in Provençal gardens.*

peeps through in places, and the seventeenth-century quarry on the property was recently reopened for the building of more retaining walls. Past and present are linked here: there are enough Roman ruins for one shady area to be designated a sculpture garden. This lies along the eastern path below the house. Nearby is a half-shrouded, laurustinus-encircled fountain with a bit of paving and a lawn chair for quiet, cool reflection in a miniature version of the typical Provençal château park. Farther on is a rough area with mixed bamboos for a children's playing ground.

Inevitably, the manor house has northern and southern aspects of equal importance, for different seasons and in different styles. The south patio has a stone balustrade and many pot and wall plants: a Mermaid rose intertwines with Sulphur Heart ivy, broadleafed *Vitis coignetiae* drapes behind. The garden furniture is dark-green painted iron, the pots overflow with white dwarf veronicas. Looking down on the

terracing of the abrupt slope below, one can see beds outlined in gray santolinas, designed like fingers around Medici-style urns, taller shrubs (some lovely *Photinia glabra* and two stately *Eriobotrya japonica*) and a central, oval space. Each finger used to have a different type of sage, but now there are more mixed plantings: acanthus, solanums, ceanothus, onopordum, white and stoechas lavenders, verbascums, perovskias, plumbagos, creamy oleanders—everything in soft pinks, mauves and whites. Hackberries provide a shaded passage. The swimming pool area is barely discernible below, its urns filled with pale pelargoniums, anthemis, and lamium cascades.

The northern façade gives onto a walled, cobbled, more formal courtyard: the "Provençal garden," where somber evergreens flank a pale fountain amid colors of rust, gold and dark green. Here are enormous terracotta urns with osmanthus, a collection of fragrant pelargoniums, nandina, and the thick, fulgent foliage of

*The astonishing garden at Val Joanis
blends wide vistas with fine detail, local tradition with foreign
inspiration in an admirable synthesis.*

Griselinia littoralis and *Arbutus unedo*. Less hardy plants can shelter here as well: daturas in pots and a feijoa by the steps in a corner. A large fig tree near the gate is entwined with a Kiftsgate rose.

Outside the gate, a crossroads links the drive with the wine cellars beyond—for this is an active wine-producing estate, where tastings may be arranged. An old stone *aiguière*, or well-cover, has been surrounded with a simple, rustic planting of catnip, centranthus, climbing roses and euphorbia. The path sloping up toward the house has many other riches, more *Vitis coignetiae* as a ground cover, jujube trees, and a blue border mixing perovskias, caryopteris, crape myrtles, catnip, wisps of white gaura, and swaths of deep blue leadwort—all plants easily grown in the south, and a very effective mixture. The main access road leading out of the domain to the hills beyond is bordered by artfully spaced cypresses with olive orchards to the south, and to the north, the famous vegetable garden, first designed by Loup de Viane.

It is hard to put into words the riches of these three broad terraces, the top two covered with formal rows of interspersed flowers and vegetables, the lowest planted with fruit trees around an iron, rose-decked *gloriette*. Cutting across the far end of all three levels runs a monumental pergola that was brought from the ruins of the Tour d'Aigues castle. Every imaginable fragrant climbing rose, jasmine, and honeysuckle has been planted along it, with glimpses of the garden outside as you pass.

Here tomatoes on bamboo stakes stand between rows of mahonia and lavender, *Salvia sclarea* backs zucchini plants, all outlined with yew cones and box lines. The latter, *Buxus balearica*, is fading in patches and will be replaced with a *Lonicera pileata* pruned to similar effect. A huge clump of *Bupleurum fruticosum* provides flowers for cutting, along with headily fragrant clerodendrons and Iceberg roses. The orchard below contains Osage orange (maclura) and white Judas trees, and is edged with a row of low-pruned plane trees (orientalis, brought from Mont Athos). Below this lowest terrace passed the drover's road in ancient times.

At 280 meters, Val Joanis has hot summers and cold winters—and an alkaline soil of eight and a half! And yet this has become a collector's garden: ivies thrive here, Glacier and Goldheart among many others, viburnums, many types of vine and ampelopsis. Madame Chancel has succeeded with many plants that could be more widely used in southern gardens without ever seeming artificial or forced—many of these indeed are native: chaste trees, bupleurums, lamiums, a variety of euphorbias, nandinas, osmanthus, *Arbutus unedo* as a pot plant, perovksias and clerodendrons, to name but a few. One may well ask where all the water comes from—but the fountains that everywhere dot the vegetation are fed by local springs, and their water is recycled.

The success of this garden comes partly from its harmonious blend of cultures: the owners are Provençal, live part of the time in London, travel to Italy (whence come ideas like the pruning

On the northern terrace (the Provençal garden) at Val Joanis, enormous Medici urns contain unusual evergreen shrubs such as osmanthus, Griselinia littoralis *and* Arbutus unedo.

and shaping of *Quercus ilex*, a practice often considered dangerous in Provence). The property is beautifully integrated into the southern landscape, and equally well into the layers of local history. But there is no doubt that it is a collector's passion that keeps enriching the plantations. A strong and reliable sense of style and much personal attention infuse this garden with its vitality. Incredibly, it is only eight years old—and Madame Chancel says that at times she is tired. But this garden is clearly, once more, "land that has been loved."

Many of the gardens presented here display, though usually on a smaller scale, a similar blending of imagination and spirit of place. Authenticity, that rare plant, grows best at these crossroads between past and future, tradition and invention. Architectural historian William Curtis agrees that the search for authenticity may produce superficial pastiche, but in the best of cases, he suggests, "It is a matter of sensing beneath the surface the memories, myths and aspirations that give a society coherence and energy." This ideal surely provides the finest model for future Provençal gardens.

One of the many fountains at Val Joanis,
a discreet and, once more, perfect blend of delight and practicality (above).
In the Val Joanis vegetable garden, tomatoes
on bamboo stakes fuse with mahonia, broadbeans and lavender
in a vast formal arrangement that superbly displays
the profusion of flowers, vegetables and fruit (following page).

239

VISITOR'S GUIDE

ADDRESSES FOR THE HEART OF PROVENCE

For those who wish to discover the surprising variety of Provençal gardens, many possibilities exist: private gardens open to the public and a wide range of municipal parks; unusual plant sources including annual fairs; wine châteaux, hotels and restaurants with lovely settings and plantings; several organized tours of gardens in the area; and finally, suppliers of garden furnishings, pottery, and so on. Listed here are those properties described in this book that the author particularly appreciated, but many others could also be mentioned.

PRIVATE GARDENS OPEN TO THE PUBLIC

ABBAYE DE SAINT-ANDRÉ
30400 Villeneuve-les-Avignon. 90 25 55 95.
Open every day April 1-October 1, 9-12:30, 13:30-19; in winter 10-12, 14:30-17.
Owner: Mlle. Roseline Bacou.
This ancient site has been turned into a model Provençal garden, a source for all who wish to explore the regional style.

DOMAINE D'ALBERTAS
13320 Bouc-Bel-Air. 42 22 29 77.
Open June 1-August 1 every day 10-12, 14-18 (Sat. 10-15); May, September and October, these hours on weekends and holidays only.
Owners: M. and Mme. Olivier Latil d'Albertas. Albertas, south of Aix-en-Provence, is one of the best known of the "bastide" gardens, now recently restored.

CHARTREUSE DU VAL-DE-LA-BÉNÉDICTION
30400 Villeneuve-les-Avignon. 90 25 05 46.
Open daily April 1-September 30, 9-18:30; winter hours 9:30-17:30.
Owner: CIRCA, a cultural association that holds a summer festival. There is a cloister garden next to the church.

CHÂTEAU D'ANSOUIS
84240 Ansouis. 90 09 82 70.
Open year round every day except Tuesdays, 14:00-18:30; closed January 1.
Owners: M. and Mme. de Sabran-Pontèves. This medieval castle in the southern Luberon has famous formal Renaissance gardens and a fascinating tour of the interior of the historic property.

CHÂTEAU DE BARBENTANE
13570 Barbentane. 90 95 51 07.
Open Easter to November 1 every day but Wednesday, 10-12, 14-18. In winter, Sundays only. Gardens may be seen only as part of the château visit.

Property of M. et Mme. Puget de Barbentane. This château just south of Avignon still belongs to the family that originally built and furnished it, and the inside visit is a rare treat. The gardens, redone in the nineteenth century, contain some unusually good sculptures.

CONSERVATOIRE DES TERRASSES EN CULTURE
Goult, 84220 Gordes. For information, tel: Association Apare in Avignon, 90 85 17 80.
Open-air museum, accessible all year.
Park at the top of the village near the ruined mill, and follow the arrows to the site, which is beautiful. It is dedicated to the preservation of old-fashioned rural economy and customs.

CHÂTEAU DE CRUSSOL D'UZES
Le Duché, 30700 Uzès. 66 22 18 96.
Owner: M. de Crussol d'Uzès.
Open: 9:30-12, 14:30-17; 18 in summer.
The château is situated in the heart of town, and usually one visits only the courtyard and waxwork display. The garden may be rented for special occasions.

FONDATION STAHLY: INTERNATIONAL CENTER OF ART AND SCULPTURE
La Verrière, 84110 Le-Haut-du-Crestet, Vaison-la-Romaine. 90 36 35 00.
Open every day but Monday, 10-12, 14-18. Best to call ahead.
Designed by architect Bruno Stahly, the foundation's park displays sculptures of his father François Stahly and others.

GOLF DES BAUX
Domaine de Manville
13250 Les-Baux-de-Provence. 90 54 40 20.
Open to members and their guests.
President: Mme. de Vilmorin.
This site is a daring synthesis between northern and southern landscaping.

HARMAS DE HENRI FABRE
84830 Sérignan-le-Comtat. 90 70 00 44.
Open every day but Tuesday and Sunday, 9-11:30, 14-18; November to March 14-16.
Manager: Mr. Teocchi.
This charming farmstead built by a famous entomologist has a lovely garden of local plants. Indoors are interesting souvenirs of its owner.

CHÂTEAU DE LA MIGNARDE
Les Pinchinnats, 13100 Aix-en-Provence. 42 96 41 86.
Visit by appointment.
Owners: M. and Mme. Séchiari.
La Mignarde is another "bastide" property in which architecture, garden sculpture and interiors have been preserved.

CHÂTEAU DE LA BARBEN
13330 La Barben. 90 55 19 12.
Château open 10-12, 14-18. Closed Tuesdays except summer.
Owner: Mr. Pons.
The garden supposedly designed by Le Nôtre is visible at all times of the year from the ramp leading up to the château and from the path below.

MAS DE LA PYRAMIDE
13210 Saint-Rémy-de-Provence. 90 92 00 81.
Open summer 9-12, 14-19; winter 10-12, 14-17.
Owner: Mr. Mauron.
This troglodyte farmstead is situated in an old Roman quarry with orchards and lavender fields. There is also a collection of antique agricultural equipment.

PUBLIC PARKS AND GARDENS

LES ALYSCAMPS
Arles. 90 49 36 36.
Open March and October: 9-12:30, 14-18. May: 9-12:30, 14-19. June through September: 8:30-19. November through February: 9-12; 14-16:30. Closed January 1, May 1, November 1, December 25.
A Roman and medieval cemetery, this shaded avenue was painted by both Van Gogh and Gauguin.

BAMBOO GARDEN OF PRAFRANCE
30140 Anduze. 66 61 70 47.
Open from Easter to November 1 every day from 9:30-12:30 and 14-18:30; from June 1 to September 24 from 9:30-19:00; in March, November and December, every day but Monday and Tuesday from 9:30-12:30 and 14-18:30.
This unusual collection of bamboos (some of which are for sale) was assembled northwest of Nîmes in the nineteenth century by Eugene Mazel. A selection of plants is for sale.

JARDIN DES LICES
Arles, Boulevard des Lices.
Open daylight hours.
The main public park in Arles, much like the one Van Gogh painted to the north of town, stands back to back with the Roman theater.

CHÂTEAU DE BEAUCAIRE
30300 Beaucaire. 66 59 47 61 (museum).
Open (park and museum) April 1-September 3 every day except Tuesday 10-12, 14:15-18:45; winter 10:15-12, 14-17:15.
Restored in a rather prosaic manner, this park is worth visiting mostly for its view and the castle.

CLOÎTRE DES CORDELIERS
13150 Tarascon. 90 91 00 07.
Open Monday to Friday, 9-12 and 14-16.
This old cloister is used by the city for
changing art exhibits, and has lovely plantings in the central courtyard.

ESPACE VAN GOGH
Rue du Président-Wilson, BP 240, 13637
Arles Cedex. 90 49 39 39.
Garden visible at all times.
Once a hospital that treated Van Gogh, this
medieval building has become a cultural
center. Its inner courtyard has been
replanted to correspond to Van Gogh's
painting of it in 1888.

JARDIN DU ROCHER DES DOMS
Pope's Palace, Avignon.
Open daylight hours.
The main public garden in Avignon, situated on an ancient hilltop site, is accessible
by a small train for those who prefer not to
walk up the steep ramps.

SQUARE AGRICOLE PERDIGUIER
41, Cours Jean-Jaurès, Avignon.
Open daylight hours.
A public square, it was redesigned in 1990-
1991 by landscapers Sébastian Giorgis,
Patrice Pierron and Jean-Louis Knidel.

JARDIN DES ARÔMES
Nyons. 75 26 04 30.
Open daylight hours.
This small but dense public park by the
river Eygue has botanical categorization
and labeling of local plants. Manager:
Jacques Lamy.

JARDIN DE LA FONTAINE
Nîmes. 66 76 73 01.
Open daylight hours.
The upper reaches of this vast garden,
which is both Roman and rococo, will be
under construction for some time.

COLLINE SAINT-EUROPE
Orange.
Open daylight hours.
This 200-acre park is situated behind and
above the famous Roman theater.

SAINT-PAUL-DE-MAUSOLE
13210 Saint-Rémy-de-Provence.
The approach lane and medieval cloister are
open during daylight hours. The surrounding
buildings still house a psychiatric clinic.

PARCS PUYMIN AND LA VILLASSE
Vaison-la-Romaine, center city near the
Office de Tourisme.
Open November to February 10-16, March

to May, September and October 10-12:30
and 14-18; June, July and August 9-12:30
and 14-19.
A public park surrounding Roman ruins on
several levels, this area contains fascinating
vestiges of Roman villas.

UNUSUAL PLANT SOURCES

Most also offer pottery and other garden
furnishings. Unfortunately, there is a sore
lack of nurseries in the region that are
both serious about quality and variety and
easily accessible to the general public.

ANTONIN
Campagne la Brousse. Les Baumettes,
84220 Gordes. 90 72 24 21.
A small nursery that also sells a good range
of pottery.

APPY
Route de Joucas, 84220 Roussillon.
90 05 62 94.
Open every afternoon.
One of the best-known nurseries of the area,
specializing in Mediterranean plants.

JARDIN DE PROVENCE
Route d'Avignon, B.P. 9, 13210. Saint-
Rémy-de-Provence. 90 92 01 57.
M. and Mme. Gérin.
Open during regular business hours.
This fascinating nursery and shop supplies
perennial Mediterranean plants, small
shrubs, rare bulbs, and garden fur-
nishings.

PÉPINIÈRES JEAN REY
1) Route de Carpentras. 84150 Jonquières.
90 70 61 13.
Open Monday to Saturday 9-12, 14-18:30.
2) Jardin Rey, Centre Commercial Conti-
nent, Orange.
Open as above, but also on Sundays.
This vast empire of nursery plants that features dozens of varieties and cultivars is
now expanding to combine expert advice
with self-service facilities.

PROVENCE ORCHIDÉES
Terre Forte, 13570 Barbentane.
90 95 50 72.
Open 12-12, 13:30-17 winter, 10-12, 14-17
summer, except holidays.
There is an exhibition of orchids and but-
terflies, and a possibility to buy orchids.

JARDINS-ESPACES VŒUX
Quartier Bouzore, 84110 Séguret.
90 46 93 34.
By appointment except for Saturday morn-

ing. Owner: Robert Vœux.
Wide range of Mediterranean plants, especially ornamental sages.

FOIRE AUX FLEURS
Held by the municipality of Tarascon every
Pentecost weekend for three days, this
event draws a wide range of plant specialists.

FOIRE DU CHÂTEAU DE BELLECOSTE
Caissargues, 30230 Bouillargues (between
Arles and Nîmes).
66 20 18 26.
This fair is held in April-May, at different
dates each year, and is organized by Mme.
du Tremblay. Many rare plants can be
found here. All year round, local produce
in great variety (wine, honey, foie gras) is
also sold on the property, which is normally open April to mid-September 9-12,
14-19; November through February 9-12,
14-18.

WINE PROPERTIES
(Gardens are usually
private but visible)

CHÂTEAU D'AQUÉRIA
30126 Tavel. 66 50 04 56.
Open usual business hours.
Owners: M. and Mme. Paul de Bez.
An elegant château-farm, this property is
visible from the highway north of Avignon.
The famous Tavel wine can be tasted and
purchased here.

CHARTREUSE DE BONPAS
84510 Caumont.
Garden generally open 9-18:30 every day.
Wine tasting and purchasing possible,
Côtes du Rhône produced by the family,
every day but Sunday.
Owners: M. and Mme. Casalis.
This is a particularly dramatic site just
near the southern Avignon freeway exit.

CHÂTEAU BAS
13116 Vernègues. 90 59 13 16.
Wine sold weekdays 8-12, 13-17; Saturdays
9-12, 14-18.
Owner: Mr. de Blanquet. Between Aix and
Cavaillon, this domain has an unusual
public promenade to a ruined Roman
temple behind the château with a view of
the formal gardens below.

CHÂTEAU D'ESTOUBLON
Maussane-les-Alpilles. 90 54 64 00.
Open usual business hours.
Owner: Mr. Lombrage.
Both wine and olive oil are sold here.

CHÂTEAU DE LA NERTHE
Châteauneuf-du-Pape. 90 83 70 11.
Open usual business hours.
Mr. Dugas, overseer.
This is certainly one of the most beautiful wine châteaux of the area.

CHÂTEAU DE VAL JOANIS
84120 Pertuis. 90 79 20 77.
Open during normal business hours.
Owners: the Chancel family.
Val Joanis possesses one of the most spectacular gardens of the region, now undergoing further changes.

HOTELS AND RESTAURANTS

CHÂTEAU D'ARPAILLARGUES
Hôtel de Marie d'Agoult. 30700 Uzès.
66 22 14 48.
Open March 15-November 1.
Owners: G. and I. Savry.
Once the property of a Romantic novelist who designed the nineteenth-century sections of the garden, this domain has vestiges from every century since Renaissance. Hotel and restaurant.

OUSTAU DE BAUMANIÈRE
Les Baux, 13520 Maussane. 90 54 33 07.
Owners and chefs: Raymond Thuilier and Jean-André Charial.
Famous above all for its cuisine, Baumanière also has a charming garden.

CHRISTIAN ÉTIENNE
10, rue Mons, 84000 Avignon. 90 86 16 50.
Fax 90 86 67 09.
This restaurant, where the owner is chef, has a lovely garden terrace in the heart of the city, next to the Pope's Palace.

CLOS DE LA VIOLETTE
10, avenue de la Violette. Aix-en-Provence.
42 23 30 71.
Closed November, March, Monday until noon and Sundays.
Owner and chef: Jean-Marc Banzo.
Situated just north of town, this quiet restaurant also has a garden terrace.

HOSTELLERIE DE CRILLON-LE-BRAVE
Place de l'Église, Crillon-le-Brave, 84410 Bédoin.
90 65 61 61. Fax 90 65 62 86.
Owner-director: Peter Chittick.
Between Carpentras and Vaison, this elegantly restored château-hôtel and restaurant has lovely terraced gardens.

RESTAURANT LES FONTAINES
11, rue Pélissane, Uzès. 66 22 12 16.
Owner: Mr. Dulaar.
This small restaurant has an interior courtyard garden in the heart of the old town.

HÔTEL D'EUROPE
12, place Crillon, 84000 Avignon.
90 82 66 92.
One of the most famous hotels and restaurants in the area, it has an extremely pleasant shaded courtyard.

HOSTELLERIE DU CHÂTEAU
Traverse Saint Pierre, Meyrargues.
42 57 50 32.
Closed November, December and January.
This medieval castle has an elegant terrace surveying the valley and the surrounding pine woods.

AUBERGE DE NOVES
13550 Noves. 90 94 19 21.
Owner: Mr. Lalleman.
This country inn has a pleasant, varied garden and a well-known restaurant.

HÔTEL LE PRIEURÉ
7, place du Chapître, Villeneuve-les-Avignon. 90 25 18 20.
Closed November to March. Owner: Mme. Jacques Mille. Chef: Serge Chenet. This "Relais-Châteaux" hotel has a lovely terrace for excellent dining and old, quite elaborate gardens.

CHÂTEAU DE ROCHEGUDE
26700 Rochegude. 75 04 81 88.
Fax 75 04 89 87.
This hotel and restaurant possesses an extensive park in which saffron grows wild.

CHÂTEAU DE ROUSSAN
13210 Saint-Rémy-de-Provence.
90 92 11 63.
Open Easter to November 15.
A famous property in the area, Roussan has an unusual and very charming garden. Hotel and restaurant.

CHÂTEAU DE SERVANE
13890 Mouriès. 90 47 50 03.
Built around an ancient shrine to Hercules, this hotel-restaurant has wonderful ancient oaks and good architectural features.

HÔTEL DU VIEUX CASTILLON
Castillon-du-Gard, 30210 Remoulins.
66 37 00 77.

Closed January to mid-March.
Another restored château, this hotel is near the Pont du Gard, and has a simple, quiet garden.

GUIDED VISITS

BOXWOOD TOURS
P.O. Box 152 Potlers Bar, Hertfordshire ENO 3NR, England.
707 37 1866. Fax 707 331 819.
In English, visits yearly. Organizer: Sue Macdonald.

CHEMINS DE PROVENCE
41, cours Jean-Jaurès, 84000 Avignon.
90 85 21 51.
This non-profit association organizes cultural visits of the *terroir* Provençal, including gardens.
Day trips (sometimes week-long trips), in French.

GARDEN TOURS
Premier Suite, Central Business Exchange, Central Milton Keynes, MK9 2EA, England.
Phone 908 609 551.
Fax 908 230 302.
English language, week-long tours.

GARDEN DECOR

LES ENFANTS DE BOISSET
30140 Anduze. 66 61 80 86.
This studio has been making Anduze vases since 1610 (they were the suppliers of the Orangery of the Château of Versailles). Their antique vases fetch extremely high prices at the local antique dealers' shops. Their contemporary production is more affordable, but customers must get on a waiting list.

POTERIE DE LA MADELEINE
Tournac, 30340 Anduze. Workshop 66 61 63 44.
Exhibition 66 61 62 12.
This is one of the specialists in the traditional glazed pottery that is found in every Provençal château.

POTERIE D'AIGUES-VIVES
30670 Aigues-Vives. 66 35 18 79.
Traditional handmade pottery, including outdoor tiles.

Facing: A map of the gardens and other points of interest mentioned in the text.

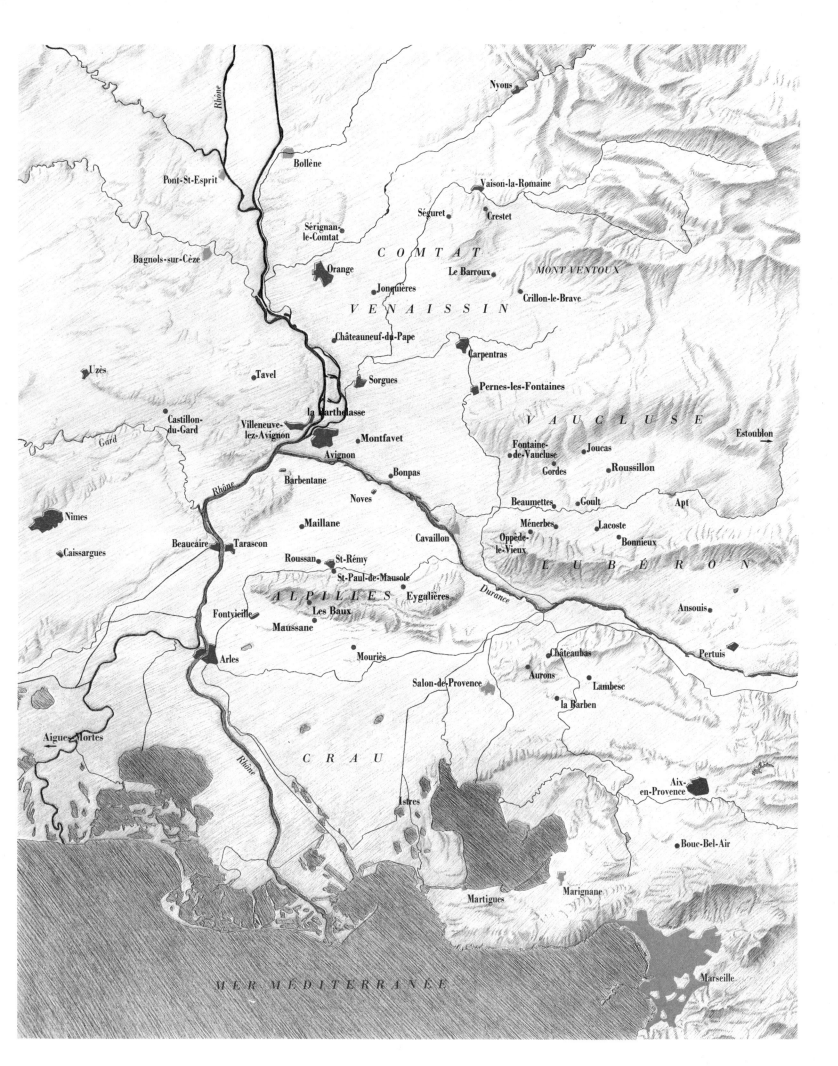

Nyous

Pont-St-Esprit

Bollène

Vaison-la-Romaine

Séguret   Crestet

Sérignan-
le-Comtat   MONT VENTOUX

Bagnols-sur-Cèze

C O M T A T

Orange   Le Barroux

Jonquières   Crillon-le-Brave

V E N A I S S I N

Châteauneuf-du-Pape

Carpentras

Uzès   Tavel   Sorgues

Pernes-les-Fontaines

la Barthelasse   V A U C L U S E   Estoublon

Castillon-   Villeneuve-   Montfavet   Fontaine-   Joucas
du-Gard   lez-Avignon   de-Vaucluse
                Avignon   Gordes   Roussillon

Gard   Bonpas

Barbentane   Beaumettes   Goult   Apt

Nîmes   Noves   Ménerbes   Lacoste

                Maillane   Oppède-   Bonnieux
                                le-Vieux

Caissargues   Cavaillon   L U B É R O N

Beaucaire   Tarascon   Durance

                Roussan   St-Rémy   Ansouis
                        St-Paul-de-Mausole

                A L P I L L E S   Eygalières   Pertuis

Fontvieille   Les Baux   Châteaubas

                Maussane   Aurons
                                Lambesc
                Mouriès   la Barben

                        Salon-de-Provence

Aigues-Mortes

                C R A U   Aix-
                                en-Provence

                Istres

                                Bouc-Bel-Air

                Martigues   Marignane

MER MÉDITERRANÉE   Marseille

COMMON PLANTS FOUND IN PROVENÇAL GARDENS

This list includes only the most common varieties and cultivars, though often others are widely available. It does not include plants that are just as common in northern climates, unless they are particularly suitable or traditional in the south. Plants are listed by their Latin names and by various common names, both British and American. Where useful, the French name is also given. Sometimes there is more than one name. Where no common names are given in English or in French, the Latin name is generally used. This list is intended to be helpful but not complete in any way.

Acacia, *Acacia dealbata*, wattle, mimosa, acacia, Fr: acacia

Acacia: common name for *Albizia*, *Robinia*, *Acacia*

Acanthus, *Acanthus mollis*

Acer, *Acer monspessulanum*, Montpelier maple, Fr: érable de Montpellier

Achillea, *Achillea filipendulina*, *A. millefolium*, Fr: achillée

Actinidia, *Actinidia chinensis*, kiwi, Fr: kiwi

Aesculus, *Aesculus x carnea*, *A. hippocastanum*, horse chestnut, Fr: marronnier

African lotus: common name for *Celtis australis*

Agapanthus, *Agapanthus africanus*, and hybrids.

Agathaea, *Agathaea coelestis* or *Felicia amelloides*

Albizia, *Albizia julibrissin*, acacia or silk tree

Allium, *Allium neapolitanum*, wild garlic, plus garden varieties

Almond: common name for *Prunus dulcis*

Althaea, *Althaea rosea* or *Alcea rosea*, hollyhock, Fr: rose tremière

Ampelopsis, *Parthenocissus quinquefolia*, Virginia creeper, *P. tricuspidata*, Boston ivy, Fr: vigne vièrge

Anthemis, *Anthemis frutescens*, *A. nobilis*, *Argyranthemum frutescens*, chamomile

Aphyllanthes, *Aphyllanthes monspeliensis*

Arbutus, *Arbutus unedo*, strawberry tree, Fr: arbousier

Artemisia, *Artemisia abrotanum*, *A. absinthium*, southernwood, wormwood, Fr: armoise, absinthe

Arundo, *Arundo donax*, giant reed, Fr: canne de Provence

Ash, mountain: common name for *Sorbus aucuparia*

Atriplex, *Atriplex halimus*, saltbush, tree purslane, Fr: arroche, halime, pourpier de mer

Baccharis, *Baccharis halimifolia*, tree groundsel, Fr: seneçon en arbre

Ballota, *Ballota pseudodictamnus*

Bay: common name for *Laurus nobilis*

Bluebeard: common name for *Caryopteris x clandonensis*

Boston ivy: common name for *Parthenocissus tricuspidata*

Bottlebrush: common name for *Callistemon*

Box: common name for *Buxus*

Broom: common name for *Spartium junceum*, *Cytisus*

Broussonetia, *Broussonetia papyrifera*, Chinese mulberry, Fr: mûrier de Chine

Buckthorn, sea: common name for *Hippophae rhamnoides*

Buddleja, *Buddleja alternifolia*, *B. colvilei*, *B. crispa*, *B. globosa*, *B. lindleyana* "Lochinch," butterfly bush, Fr: arbre à papillons

Bupleurum, *Bupleurum fruticosum*, Fr: buplèvre

Butterfly bush: common name for *Buddleia*

Buxus, *Buxus balearica*, *B. sempervirens* "Suffruticosa," box, Fr: buis

Callistemon, *Callistemon laevis*, bottlebrush

Campsis, *Campsis radicans*, Fr: trompette de Jéricho, jasmin de Virginie

Cape fuchsia: common name for *Phygelius capensis*

Caper: common name for *Capparis spinosa*

Capparis, *Capparis spinosa*, caper, Fr: caprier

Cardoon: common name for *Cynara cardunculus*

Caryopteris, *Caryopteris x clandonensis*, Bluebeard

Castanea, *Castanea sativa*, Fr: châtaignier

Catalpa, *Catalpa bignonioides*

Catananche, *Catananche caerulea*, blue cupidone, Fr: cupidone

Ceanothus, *Ceanothus arboreus*, *C. burfordiensis*, *C. x delileanus*, *C. impressus*, *C. x pallidus*, *C. thyrsiflorus*

Cedar: common name for *Cedrus*

Cedrus, *Cedrus atlantica*, *C. deodara*, *C. libani*, cedar, Fr: cèdre

Celtis, *Celtis australis*, African lotus, hackberry or nettle tree, Fr: micocoulier

Centranthus, *Centranthus ruber*, false valerian, Fr: valériane

Ceratostigma, *Ceratostigma larpentae* or *C. plumbaginoides*, leadwort, *C. willmottianum*, Fr: dentelaire

Cercis, *Cercis siliquastrum*, Judas tree or redbud, Fr: arbre de Judée

Cestrum, *Cestrum aurantiacum*, *C. nocturnum*

Chamaerops, *Chamaerops humilis*, dwarf fan palm

Chaste tree: common name for *Vitex agnus-castus*

Chestnut: common name for *Castanea sativa*

Choisya, *Choisya ternata*, mock orange, Mexican orange, Fr: oranger du Mexique

Cineraria, *Cineraria maritima* or *Senecio cineraria*

Cistus, *Cistus aguilari*, *C. albidus*, *C. x corbariensis*, *C. crispus x* "Sunset" *purpureus*, *C. monspeliensis*, rock rose, Fr: ciste

Clerodendrum, *Clerodendrum bungei*, *C. trichotomum*

Colutea, *Colutea arborescens*, Fr: baguenaudier

Convolvulus, *Convolvulus cneorum*, *C. mauritanicus*

Coronilla, *Coronilla emerus*, *C. glauca*

Cotinus, *Cotinus coggygria*, smoke tree, Venetian sumach, Fr: arbre à perruque

Cotton lavender: common name for *Santolina*

Crape myrtle: common name for *Lagerstroemia indica*

Cupidone, blue: common name for *Catananche caerulea*

Cupressus, *Cupressus arizonica*, *C. dupreziana*, *C. sempervirens*

Curry plant: common name for *Helichrysum angustifolium*

Cynara, *Cynara cardunculus*, cardoon, Fr: cardon

Cypress: common name for *Cupressus*

Daisy bush: common name for *Olearia*

Datura, *Datura* hybrids, or *Brugmansia*

Dead nettle: common name for *Lamium*

Delosperma, *Delosperma cooperi*

Desmodium: see *Lespedeza*

Dimorphotheca, *Osteospermum* or *Dimorphotheca barberae*, *D. pluvialis*, *Diospyros kaki*, persimmon, Fr: plaqueminier

Donkey pepper: common name for *Satureja montana*

Dusty miller: common name for *Cineraria*

Echinops, *Echinops ritro*, Fr: chardon bleu

Elaeagnus, *Elaeagnus angustifolia*, oleaster, Russian olive, Fr: olivier de bohème; *E. x ebbingei*, *E. macrophylla*, *E. pun-*

gens, *E. umbellata*, Fr: chalef
Erigeron, *Erigeron karvinskianus* or *E. mucronatus*
Eriobotrya, *Eriobotrya japonica*, loquat, Fr: neflier du Japon
Eryngium, *Eryngium alpinum*, sea holly, Fr: panicaut
Erysimum, *Erysimum linifolium* or *E. torulosum*
Eucalyptus, *Eucalyptus gunnii*, *E. pauciflora niphophila*, gum tree
Euphorbia, *Euphorbia characias*, *E. polychroma*, *E. robbiae*, *E. seguieriana niciana*
Euryops, *Euryops abrotanifolius* or *E. pectinatus*

Fan palm, dwarf: common name for *Chamaerops humilis*
Felicia, *Felicia amelloides* or *Agathaea coelestis*, Fr: aster du Cap
Fennel: common name for *Foeniculum* vulgare
Ficus, *Ficus carica*, fig, Fr: figuier
Fig: common name for *Ficus*
Foeniculum, *Foeniculum vulgare dulce*, fennel, Fr: fenouil
Foxglove tree: common name for *Paulownia imperialis* or *F. tomentosa*
Fremontodendron, *Fremontodendron californicum*

Garlic, wild: common name for *Allium neapolitanum*
Gaura, *Gaura lindheimeri*
Genista, *Genista lydia*, *G. prostrata*, *G. scorpius*
Germander, shrubby: common name for *Teucrium fruticans*
Gleditsia, *Gleditsia triacanthos*, *G. inermis*, Fr: févier
Glory bush: common name for *Tibouchina urvilleana*
Gum tree: common name for *Eucalyptus*

Hackberry: common name for *Celtis australis*
Hebe, *Hebe x andersonii*, *H. armstrongii*, and hybrids
Helichrysum, *Helichrysum angustifolium*, curry plant
Heliotrope, winter: common name for *Petasites fragrans*
Hibiscus, *Hibiscus syriacus*
Hippophae, *Hippophae rhamnoides*, sea buckthorn, Fr: argousier
Holly, sea: common name for *Eryngium*
Hollyhock: common name for *Althaea rosea* or *Alcea rosea*
Horse chestnut: common name for *Aesculus hippocastanum*

Hypericum, *Hypericum calycinum*, *H. hookerianum*, *H. inodorum*, *H. x moserianum*, Fr: millepertuis
Hyssop: common name for *Hyssopus*
Hyssopus, *Hyssopus officinalis*

Indian bean tree: common name for *Catalpa bignonioides*

Jasmine, confederate or star: common name for *Trachelospermum jasminoides*
Jasminum, *Jasminum officinale*, *J. grandiflorum*, *J. mesnyi*, *J. nudiflorum*
Judas tree: common name for *Cercis*
Jujube: common name for *Ziziphus vulgaris*
Juniper: common name for *Juniperus*
Juniperus, *Juniperus communis juniper*, Fr: genevrier commun; *J. oxycedrus*, Fr: cade, phoenicia

Kiwi: common name for *Actinidia chinensis*
Koelreuteria, *Koelreuteria paniculata*, Fr: savonnier

Lagerose: common name for *Lagerstroemia indica*
Lagerstroemia, *Lagerstroemia indica*, crape myrtle, lagerose or summer lilac, Fr: lilas des Indes
Lamium, *Lamium galeobdolon*, *L. maculatum*, dead nettle
Lantana, *Lantana sellowiana* and hybrids
Laurel: common name for *Laurus nobilis*
Laurustinus: common name for *Viburnum tinus*
Lavandula, *Lavandula* "Alba," *L. angustifolia et cultivars*, *L. dentata*, *L. nana*, *L. officinalis*, *L. spica*, *L. stoechas*, *L. "Vera"*
Lavatera, *Lavatera arborea*, *L. maritima*, *L. olbia*, *L. thuringiaca*, tree mallow, Fr: lavatère
Lavender: common name for *Lavandula*
Lavender cotton: common name for *Santolina*
Leadwort: common name for *Ceratostigma*
Lentisk: common name for *Pistacia lentiscus*
Lespedeza, *Lespedeza formosa*, *L. thunbergii*, or *L. desmodium*
Lime: common name for *Tilia*
Linden: common name for *Tilia*
Lippia, *Lippia citriodora* or *Aloysia triphylla*; lemon verbena, Fr: verveine citronelle; *Lippia repens* or *Phyla nodiflora*
Loquat: common name for *Eriobotrya japonica*

Maclura, *Maclura pomifera*, Osage orange
Mallow, tree: common name for *Lavatera*
Maple: common name for *Acer*
Mastic: common name for *Pistacia lentiscus*

Mexican orange: common name for *Choisya ternata*
Mimosa: common name for *Acacia*
Mock orange: common name for *Choisya ternata*, *Pittosporum tobira*, or *Philadelphus*
Morus, *Morus alba*, *M. kagayamae*, Fr: mûrier platane; *M. nigra*, *M. rubra*, white, black, red mulberry, Fr: mûrier
Mulberry: common name for *Morus* or *Broussonetia*
Myrtle: common name for *Myrtus*
Myrtus, *Myrtus communis*, *M. tarentina*, myrtle, Fr: myrte

Nerium, *Nerium oleander*, oleander, Fr: laurier rose
Nettle tree: common name for *Celtis australis*

Oak: common name for *Quercus*
Oleander: common name for *Nerium oleander*
Olearia, *Olearia x haastii*, *O. solandri*, daisy bush
Oleaster: common name for *Elaeagnus angustifolia*
Olive, sweet: common name for *Osmanthus fragrans*
Olive: common name for *Olea europaea*
Osage orange: common name for *Maclura*
Osmanthus, *Osmanthus fragrans*, sweet olive, *O. heterophyllus*

Pagoda tree: common name for *Sophora japonica*
Passiflora, *Passiflora caerulea*, Fr: passiflore
Passion flower: common name for *Passiflora*
Paulownia, *Paulownia imperialis* or *P. tomentosa*, foxglove tree or princess tree
Persimmon: common name for *Diospyros kaki*
Petasites, *Petasites fragrans*, winter heliotrope
Phillyrea, *Phillyrea angustifolia*, *P. media*
Phlomis, *Phlomis fruticosa*, *P. russeliana*
Photinia, *Photinia x fraseri*, *P. glabra*, *P. errulata* or *P. serratifolia*
Phygelium, *Phygelius capensis*, cape fuchsia
Pine: common name for *Pinus*
Pinus, *Pinus laricio*, Corsican pine, *P. maritima*, maritime pine, *P. nigra*, Austrian pine, *P. pinea*, parasol pine, stone pine
Pistacia, *Pistachia lentiscus*, mastic or lentisk, Fr: lentisque
Pittosporum, *Pittosporum tenuifolium*, *P. tobira*, mock orange.
Plane: common name for *Platanus*

Platanus, *Platanus x acerifolia*, *P. orientalis*
Plumbago, *Plumbago capensis* or *Cerato-stigma plumbaginoides*
Podranea, *Podranea ricasoliana*
Pomegranate: common name for *Punica granatum*
Princess flower: common name for *Tibouchina urvilleana*
Princess tree: common name for *Paulownia imperialis* or *P. tomentosa*
Punica, *Punica granatum*, pomegranate, Fr: grenadier

Quercus, *Quercus coccifera*, kermes oak, Fr: chène kermès; *Q. ilex*, holm oak, Fr: chène vert or yeuse; *Q. pubescens*, white oak, Fr: chène blanc; *Q. suber*, cork oak, Fr: chène liège

Redbud: common name for *Cercis*
Reed, giant: common name for *Arundo donax*
Rhamnus, *Rhamnus alaternus*, Fr: alaterne
Rhaphiolepis, *Rhaphiolepis x delacourii*
Rhus, *Rhus coriaria*, *R. typhina*, sumach
Robinia, *Robinia pseudoacacia*, false acacia, locust, black or honey locust; Fr: acacia, robinier
Rock rose: common name for *Cistus*
Romneya, *Romnyea coulteri*, Fr: pavot blanc
Rosemary: common name for *Rosmarinus*
Rosmarinus, *Rosmarinus officinalis*, *R. angustifolius*, *R. corsicus* "Prostratus", *R. repens*
Rowan: common name for *Sorbus aucuparia*
Rue: common name for *Ruta*
Russian olive: common name for *Elaeagnus angustifolia*
Russian sage: common name for *Perovskia atriplicifolia*
Ruta, *Ruta graveolens*, rue, Fr: rue

Sage: common name for *Salvia*
Saltbush: common name for *Atriplex halimus*
Salvia, *Salvia argentea*, *S. azurea*, *S. grahamii*, *S. greggii*, *S. guaranitica*, *S. haematodes*, *S. involucrata*, *S. leucantha*, *S. microphylla*, *S. nemorosa*, *S. officinalis*, *S. pratensis*, *S. rutilans*, *S. uliginosa*, *S. verticillata*
Santolina, *Santolina chamaecyparissus*, *S. viridis*, lavender cotton
Satureja, *Satureja montana*, winter savory, donkey pepper, Fr: sarriette, Provençal: pèbre d'ase
Savory, winter: common name for *Satureja montana*
Scholar tree, Japanese: common name for *Sophora japonica*
Senecio, *Senecio greyi*
Silk tree: common name for *Albizia julibrissin*
Smoke tree: common name for *Cotinus*
Solanum, *Solanum jasminoides*, *S. rantonnetti*, *S. wendlandii*
Sophora, *Sophora japonica*, Japanese scholar tree, pagoda tree
Sorbus, *Sorbus aucuparia*, mountain ash, rowan, Fr: sorbier torminalis, alisier
Southernwood: common name for *Artemisia*
Spurge: common name for *Euphorbia*
Stachys, *Stachys lanata* or *S. byzantina*
Sternbergia, *Sternbergia sicula*
Strawberry tree: common name for *Arbutus unedo*
Sumach: common name for *Rhus*
Sumach, Venetian: common name for *Cotinus*
Summer lilac: common name for *Lagerstroemia indica* or *Ceanothus*

Tamarisk: common name for *Tamarix*
Tamarix, *Tamarix africana*, *T. gallica*, *T. pentandra*, tamarisk

Teucrium, *Teucrium chamaedrys*, *T. fruticans*
Thyme: common name for *Thymus vulgaris*
Tibouchina, *Tibouchina semidecandra*, *T. urvilleana*, glory bush, princess flower
Tilia, *Tilia platyphyllos*, *T. tomentosa*, lime, linden, Fr: tilleul
Trachelospermum, *Trachelospermum jasminoides*, confederate or star jasmine, Fr: jasmin étoilé de Chine
Tree groundsel: common name for *Baccharis halimifolia*
Tree purslane: common name for *Atriplex halimus*
Trumpet vine: common name for *Campsis*

Valerian, false valerian: common name for *Centranthus ruber*
Verbena, lemon: common name for *Lippia citriodora*, or *Aloysia triphylla*
Verbena, *Verbena peruviana*, *V. radicans*, *V. rigida* or *V. venosa*, *V. tenax*, Fr: verveine
Veronica, *Veronica teucrium*, *V. longifolia*
Viburnum, *Viburnum tinus*, laurustinus, Fr: laurier tin
Viola, *Viola cornuta*, *V. odorata*
Violet: common name for *Viola*
Virginia creeper: common name for *Parthenocissus quinquefolia*
Vitex, *Vitex agnus-castus*, chaste tree, Fr: gattelier, arbre à poivre
Vittadinia: common name for *Erigeron mucronatus* or *V. karvinskianus*

Wattle: common name for *Acacia*
Wisteria, *Wisteria sinensis*, *W. floribunda*, Fr: glycine
Wormwood: common name for *Artemisia*

Yucca, *Yucca gloriosa*

Zizyphus, *Zizyphus vulgaris*, *Z. jujube*, Fr: jujubier

BIBLIOGRAPHY

GARDEN HISTORY:

FUSTIER-DAUTIER, Nerte. *Les Bastides de Provence et leurs jardins.* Serg/Berger-Levrault, Paris, 1977.

GRIMAL, Pierre. *Les jardins romains.* Fayard, Paris, 1984.

GROMORT, Georges. *L'Art des jardins.* Ch. Massin, Paris, n.d.

HOBHOUSE, Penelope. *Garden Style.* Little, Brown and Co., Boston and Toronto, 1988.

Jardins de Méditerranée. Exhibition catalogue, CIRCA in collaboration with Radio Monte-Carlo, La Chartreuse, Villeneuve-les-Avignon, July 1980.

JELLICOE, Geoffrey and Susan; GOODE, Patrick; LANCASTER, Michael. *The Oxford Companion to Gardens.* Oxford University Press, Oxford, 1986.

LE DANTEC, Denise and Jean-Pierre. *Le Roman des Jardins de France.* Plon, Paris, 1987.

LEQUENNE, Fernand. *Olivier de Serres: agronome et soldat de Dieu.* Berger-Levraut, Paris, 1983.

MARCEL, Adrien. "Jardins avignonnais du 17e et 18e siècle," *Annales de l'Académie du Vaucluse.* 2e Série, 1918-20, pp. 298-323.

MOORE, Charles W.; MICHELL, William J.; TURNBULL, William, Jr. *The Poetics of Gardens.* MIT Press, Cambridge, Mass., n.d.

PECHERE, René. "Trois Jardins de Provence et leurs parterres de buis." *Vieilles Maisons françaises.* August 1983, no. 98, pp. 76-77.

RACINE and BINET. *Gardens of Provence and the Côte d'Azur.* MIT Press, Cambridge, Mass., 1989.

SABRAN-PONTEVES, La Duchesse de. *Bon sang ne peut mentir.* J. Clattès, Paris, 1987.

SOLOMON, Barbara Stauffacher. *Green Architecture and the Agrarian Garden.* Rizzoli, New York, 1988.

WHARTON, Edith. *Italian Villas and Their Gardens.* DaCapo, New York, 1976.

NATURAL HISTORY AND PRACTICAL GARDENING:

CREASY, Rosalind. *The Complete Book of Edible Landscaping.* Sierra Club Books, San Francisco, 1982.

DANESCH, O. and Reisigl, H. *Flore Méditerranéenne.* Payot, Lausanne, n.d.

GUEIDAN, E. *Le Jardinier provençal: traité de culture pratique pour le midi de la France.* Tacussel, Marseille, 1974.

Guide de la nature en France. Preface Paul-Emile Victor. Bordas, Paris, 1979.

HARANT, H. and Jarry, D. *Guide du naturaliste du Midi de la France.* 2 vols. Delachaux and Niestlé, Neuchâtel, Switzerland, 1973.

LANCASTER, Roy and Vicomte de Noäilles. *Plantes de jardins méditerranéens.* Larousse, Paris, 1977.

LATYMER, Hugo. *The Mediterranean Gardener.* Frances Lincoln, London, 1990.

MENSIES, Yves. *Mediterraean Gardening: A Practical Handbook.* 1991.

PHILLIPS, Roger. *Fleurs de Méditerranée.* Bordas, Paris, 1988.

POLUNIN, O. and HUXLEY, A. *Flowers of the Mediterranean.* Chatto and Windus, London, 1981.

RACINE, Michel. *Le Guide des Jardins de France.* Guides Hachette, Paris, 1990.

ROUSSARD, R. and CUISANCE, P. *Arbres et Arbustes d'ornement des Régions tempérés et méditerranéens.* J. B. Baillière-Lavoisier, Paris, 1984.

GUIDE BOOKS AND TRAVEL WRITING:

ALIQUOT, Hervé. *Avignon pas à pas.* Horvath, Roanne Le Coteau, 1985.

ALIQUOT, Hervé. *Les Alpilles.* Aubanel, Avignon, 1989.

BYK, Christian. *Guide des jardins de Provence et de Côte d'Azur.* Berger-Levrault and Nice Matin, 1988.

FORBES, Leslie. *A Taste of Provence.* Little, Brown and Co., Boston and Toronto, 1988.

JACOBS, Michael. *A Guide to Provence.* Viking Penguin, London, 1988.

JAMES, Henry. *A Little Tour in France.* Oxford University Press, Oxford, 1984.

MAYLE, Peter. *A Year in Provence.* Hamish Hamilton, London, 1989.

MOORE, Carey and Julian. *Views from a French Farmhouse.* Pavillon, London, 1985.

POPE-HENNESSY, James. *Aspects of Provence.* Penguin Travel Library, London, 1988.

RACINE, Michel. *Le Guide des Jardins de France.* Guides Hachette, Paris, 1990.

LITERATURE AND ART:

BARBIER, Elizabeth. *Les Gens de Mogador.* 6 vols., Juillard, Livre de Poche, 1952.

BOSCO, Henri. *Le Trestoulas* and *L'Habitant de Sivergues.* Gallimard, Paris, 1935.

BRINK, André. *The Wall of the Plague.* Fontana, London, 1984.

COLETTE, *Break of Day.* Trans. Enid McLeod. Farrar, Straus and Giroux, New York, 1961.

COLETTE, *The Vagabond.* Trans. Enid McLeod. Farrar, Straus and Giroux, New York, 1955.

DAUDET, Alphonse. *Letters from My Mill.* Trans. Edward Ardizzone. Penguin, Middlesex, 1978.

DURRELL, Lawrence. *The Avignon Quintet,* Penguin, Middlesex, 1984.

DURRELL, Lawrence. *Spirit of Place: Letters and Essays on Travel.* Leete's Island Books, New Haven, Conn., 1969.

FORD, Ford Madox. *Provence.* Ecco Press, New York, 1979.

GIONO, Jean. *Manosque-des-Plateaux suivi de Poème de l'olive.* Gallimard, Paris, 1986.

MISTRAL, Frédéric. *Memoires.* Trans.

George Wickes. New Directions, New York, 1988.

PAGNOL, Marcel. *Memories of Childhood*. Trans. Rita Barisse, North Point Press, Berkeley, California, 1986.

PAGNOL, Marcel. *The Water of the Hills: Jean de Florette and Manon of the Springs*. Trans. W. E. van Heyningen, Northpoint Press, Berkeley, California, 1988.

PICKVANCE, Ronald. *Van Gogh in Arles*. Metropolitan Museum of Art, New York, 1984.

ROSKILL, Mark. *The Letters of Vincent Van Gogh*. Atheneum, New York, 1963.

STENDHAL, *Memoirs of a Tourist*. Trans. Allan Seager, Northwestern University Press, Chicago, 1962.

STONE, Irving, ed. *Letters to Theo*. Signet, New York, 1969.

THOMPSON, David. *Petrarch: An Anthology*. Harper and Row, New York, 1971.

TOURNIER, Michel. *Petites proses*. Gallimard Folio, Paris, 1986.

WENTINCK, Charles. *Provence: mythes et réalités*. Editions Bernard Coutaz, Arles, 1989.

WICKES, George, ed. "Readings for Innocents Abroad," Anthology of photocopied literary excerpts, Avignon, Spring 1985.

HISTORY:

ALIQUOT, Hervé. *Les Palais cardinalices hors les murs d'Avignon au XIVe siècle*. Thesis, Université d'Aix-en-Provence, 1983.

Atlas historique: Provence, Comtat Venaissin, Principauté de Monaco, Pincipauté d'Orange, Comté de Nice. Armand Colin, Paris, 1969.

BAILLY, Robert. *Châteaux historiques vauclusiens*. Bailly, Imp. F. Orta, Avignon, n.d.

BARATIER, Edouard, dir. *Histoire de la Provence*. Privat, Toulouse, 1969.

BRAUDEL, Fernand. *L'Identité de la France*. 4 vols., Arthaud-Flammarion, Paris, 1986.

CHARLTON, D. G. *New Images of the Natural in France*. Cambridge University Press, Cambridge, 1984.

CLÉBERT, Jean-Paul. *Provence antique*, 2 vols., Robert Laffont, Paris, 1970.

COULET, Noël. "La Naissance de la Bastide provençale," *Géographie historique du village et de la maison rurale: actes du colloque de Bazas (Gironde)*. Nos. 19-21; Oct. 1978, 1979.

GIRARD, Joseph. *Evocation du vieil Avignon*. Editions de Minuit, Paris, 1958.

ROLLET, Pierre. *La Vie quotidienne en Provence au temps de Mistral*. Hachette, Paris, 1972.

RURAL LIFE:

ALGOUD, Henri. *Sur la Route des mas et des bastides*. Editions Detaille, Marseille, 1958.

BENOIT, Fernand. *La Provence et le Comtat Venaissin: arts et traditions populaires*. Aubanel, Avignon, 1975.

BROMBERGER, Christian; LACROIX; RAULIN, Henri. *L'Architecture rurale en Provence*. Berger-Levrault, Paris, 1980.

COSTE, Pierre, and MARTEL, Pierre. *Pierre sèche en Provence*. Alpes de Lumière, Fourcalquier, 1985.

LIVET, R. *Habitat rural et structures agraires en basse Provence*. Editions Ophrys, Aix-en-Provence, 1962.

MASSOT, J-L. *Maisons rurales et vie paysanne en Provence*. Serg, Paris, 1975.

MOULIN, Pierre; LEVEC, Pierre; DANNENBERG, Linda. *Pierre Deux's French Country: A Style and Source Book*. Octopus Books, Clarkson Potter, New York, 1984. In French, *L'Art de vivre en Provence*. Flammarion, Paris, 1986.

PLUMMER, Henry. "The Unique Hilltowns of France," *Architecture*, September 1986.

LANDSCAPE AND SITES:

A la découvrte de la Garrigue. Centre régional de documentation pédagogique, Montpellier, 1987.

AMBROISE, Régis; FRAPA, Pierre; GIORGIS, Sébastien. *Paysages de terrasses*. Edisud, Aix-en-Provence, 1989.

CURTIS, William J. R. "Towards an Authentic Regionalism," MIMAR 19 (Singapore: Aga Khan Publications), January 1986.

JACQUEMONT, Guy; Galant, Patrick. *Le grand livre des Côtes du Rhône*. Chêne, Paris, 1988.

Merveilles des Châteaux de Provence. Preface Duc de Castries. Hachette, Paris, 1965.

PITTE, Jean-Robert. *Histoire du paysage français*. 2 vols., Tallandier, Paris, 1983.

TRUC, Georges. *Ressources minérales du Vaucluse: des matériaux et des hommes*. Chambre de Commerce et d'Industrie d'Avignon et de Vaucluse, Avignon, 1979.

U.E.R. d'Histoire, Université de Provence. *Campagnes méditerranéennes, permanances et mutations*. CRDP Marseille, 1977.

YAPP, Peter, ed. *The Travellers' Dictionary of Quotation*. Routledge and Kegan Paul, London, Boston, Melbourne and Henley, 1983.

ACKNOWLEDGEMENTS

Many people have been most generous with their help, not least the garden owners themselves. I would particulary like to express gratitude to the late Elizabeth d'Anselme, for her careful reading of the early stages of the manuscript; for advice and sources, the following have been very hepful: Hervé Aliquot, author of numerous books on Provence; Pierre de Brion, Yves Coutarel, Émile Garcin, Françoise Gérin, Paul Hanbury and Robartus Shootemayer, Nicole Martin-Raget, Thérèse Moyne, Michel Racine, Jean-Marie Rey, François de Roubin, Michel Semini, Anne Simonet. For their patience and encouragement in the writing, warm thanks to Annie François and Madeleine Deschamps.

The publisher joins the author in thanking all the owners who opened their gardens to Louisa Jones and Vincent Motte during these two years. Special thanks go to Carolan and Terence Conran, Ann Cox Chambers, the Baroness of Waldner, Lillian Williams and all persons who communicated their passion for the gardens of Provence and made the preparation of this book a constant pleasure. They include Marguerite Dumas, Joe Fitchett, Franz and Marie-Claire Mayer, Gérard-Julien Salvy, Roger Vergé, Walter and Patricia Wells, and Larry and Joan Wylie.

I N D E X